BEING NATURE

"A milestone in contemporary Buddhism. Nisker grounds the Buddha's teachings in discoveries made by the neural and evolutionary sciences. I dare you to find a book on science that is so personal or a book on meditation that is so funny and forgiving."

JOANNA MACY, PH.D., ENVIRONMENTAL ACTIVIST,
BUDDHIST SCHOLAR, AND AUTHOR OF
A WILD LOVE FOR THE WORLD

"Wes Nisker is one of my all-time favorite teachers. With tremendous warmth and wit, he shows us a path to profound inner peace that is grounded in both science and the liberating insights of the Buddha. Each page of this timeless classic shines with humor, beautiful and clear writing, fascinating research —and the heartfelt invitation to find lasting love and happiness right in the middle of life itself."

RICK HANSON, PH.D.,
AUTHOR OF *BUDDHA'S BRAIN*

"This book brings to life an ancient meditative wisdom that has the deepest of relevance to our lives as individuals and as a species. It is a masterful look at who we are and how great our potential is to realize our true nature here and now, before this fleeting moment we call 'our' life dissolves back into all life and the opportunity of a lifetime is missed."

JON KABAT-ZINN, FOUNDER OF
MINDFULNESS-BASED STRESS REDUCTION

"One of the best efforts yet to bring together meditators and scientists. It is an instrument for our greater joy and achievements."

THICH NHAT HANH (1926–2022), ZEN MASTER
AND AUTHOR OF *PEACE IS EVERY STEP*

"With careful and heartfelt reflections, Wes Nisker, drawing upon Buddhist practices, lays out a path whereby humanity can ride the truths of science into a sublime and joyful freedom. This book is truly a healing and historic achievement."

BRIAN SWIMME, PH.D., PROFESSOR OF EVOLUTIONARY COSMOLOGY AT THE CALIFORNIA INSTITUTE OF INTEGRAL STUDIES AND AUTHOR OF *THE UNIVERSE IS A GREEN DRAGON*

"A joy to read—an illuminating and often humorous synthesis of ancient Buddhist understanding and present-day discoveries in biology and cognitive science. Wes Nisker grounds the theory in his own deep experience of meditation, offering a wealth of practical mind-exploring exercises that transform knowledge into wisdom. It is a wonderful book."

JOSEPH GOLDSTEIN, COFOUNDER OF THE INSIGHT MEDITATION SOCIETY AND AUTHOR OF *ONE DHARMA: THE EMERGING WESTERN BUDDHISM*

"What delight and illumination are contained in these pages! Science (particularly evolutionary biology) and religion have lacked a common language in which to converse—Wes Nisker's book manages to articulate a new dialect that not only syncretizes a host of important principles but also is music to the ear."

AJAHN AMARO, ABBOT OF AMARAVATI BUDDHIST MONASTERY AND AUTHOR OF *AN INTRODUCTION TO THE LIFE AND TEACHINGS OF AJAHN CHAH*

"Nisker's prose has always been engaging, but here he writes with greater maturity, without sacrificing the impishness that has characterized his earlier work. In time, people will consider *Being Nature* as groundbreaking a work as an earlier classic of interdisciplinary synthesis, *The Tao of Physics*."

YOGA JOURNAL

BEING NATURE

A Down-to-Earth Guide to the
Four Foundations of Mindfulness

A Sacred Planet Book

Wes "Scoop" Nisker

Inner Traditions
Rochester, Vermont

Inner Traditions
One Park Street
Rochester, Vermont 05767
www.InnerTraditions.com

SUSTAINABLE FORESTRY INITIATIVE · Certified Sourcing · www.sfiprogram.org · SFI-00854

Text stock is SFI certified

Sacred Planet Books are curated by Richard Grossinger, Inner Traditions editorial board member and cofounder and former publisher of North Atlantic Books. The Sacred Planet collection, published under the umbrella of the Inner Traditions family of imprints, includes works on the themes of consciousness, cosmology, alternative medicine, dreams, climate, permaculture, alchemy, shamanic studies, oracles, astrology, crystals, hyperobjects, locutions, and subtle bodies.

Cataloging-in-Publication Data for this title is available from the Library of Congress

ISBN 978-1-64411-537-4 (print)
ISBN 978-1-64411-538-1 (ebook)

Printed and bound in the United States by Lake Book Manufacturing, Inc. The text stock is SFI certified. The Sustainable Forestry Initiative® program promotes sustainable forest management.

10 9 8 7 6 5 4 3 2 1

Text design and layout by Virginia Scott Bowman
This book was typeset in Garamond Premier Pro and Gill Sans with Gandhi Serif and Exo 2 used as display typefaces.

To send correspondence to the author of this book, mail a first-class letter to the author c/o Inner Traditions • Bear & Company, One Park Street, Rochester, VT 05767, and we will forward the communication, or contact the author directly at **https://wesnisker.com**.

❧

*To the single-celled organism known as LUCA,
the "last universal common ancestor,"
and all beings who followed,
including my parents, my daughter,
and of course, YOU.*

Contents

Foreword

꙰ ꙰

Jack Kornfield, PhD

Albert Einstein famously exhorted us to step out of the optical delusion of separateness and widen our circle of compassion.

Today we know how important this is as we face global pandemics, rising oceans and climate crisis, the increasing disparity between rich and poor, and the calls for racial, social, and economic justice.

The question is how can we do this? How can we step out of the optical delusion of separateness? How do we become wise stewards of our lives and true lovers of our Earth?

You have in your hands a brilliant answer. *Being Nature* is a unique work: profoundly scientific and equally poetic, grounded in earth-based wisdom and equally spiritual. It is also funny and fresh and startlingly new.

Like the corpus callosum that links the left and right hemispheres of the brain, *Being Nature* links deep ways of knowing, those from the sciences of biology, ecology, and physics and those from the profound contemplative knowings of the heart. Most importantly, it is a visionary workbook, an inner journey and guide to use in your own body, heart, and mind to awaken new understanding and universal compassion.

Take a deep breath right now. Pause. Turn your attention to the mystery of your human life and your singular uniqueness among all beings. Now notice how your bodily life depends on constantly exchanging gas, breathing the same air with all breathing beings. We are an inter-breathing organism. Relax into wonder.

This is a tiny first step in how to read this masterful text. In his fresh way, Wes will lead you step by step through dozens of practices and reflections to open your mind and engage your heart. Universal in nature, these illuminating practices are drawn from the core of the Buddha's path to awakening. They follow the famed and powerful tools of the Foundations of Mindfulness which systematically explore our nature as part of the nature of it all. The body, the elements, states of mind, feelings, consciousness, birth and death, and our interrelations with society, environment, and all life are all included.

Take your time with this book. Let it percolate, season you as you read. Try each practice and reflection in turn. Each is a skillful means to lovingly deconstruct your separateness and restore the lost pearl of your freedom. Each has a power to dissolve the illusions of separateness and open you to a wise, spacious, and compassionate consciousness.

Wes Nisker has offered you this special gift, deep, refreshingly charming, immensely creative. It is an invitation to awaken.

Enjoy and embody.

With metta and blessings,
Jack Kornfield
Spirit Rock Meditation Center, 2021

JACK KORNFIELD is one of the key teachers to introduce mindfulness practice to the West. Trained as a Buddhist monk, he is a founder of Spirit Rock Center and The Insight Meditation Society. A psychologist, husband, grandfather, and activist, he is the author of sixteen books.

Buddhas use countless numbers of expedient means, various causes and conditions, and words of simile and parable to expound the doctrines for the sake of living beings. And these living beings, by listening to the doctrines of the Buddhas, are all eventually able to attain wisdom embracing all species

THE LOTUS SUTRA

PROLOGUE

❧ ᭢

Who Goes There?

T he inspiration for this book goes back at least as far as my first
meditation retreat, which took place in 1970 in the village of
Bodhgaya, India. The temple in which I began to practice this ancient
art was just a few minutes' walk from the Bodhi tree where more than
twenty-five hundred years earlier the Buddha is said to have sat down
and found liberation. I was part of a wave of young Americans and
Europeans who had traveled to Asia in a somewhat confused, romantic
search for new ways of understanding life and living it.

When I sat down to meditate at that first retreat, I was already
twenty-eight years old and had a liberal arts degree from a fine American
college and several years of graduate school, and I had undergone some
Freudian and gestalt psychotherapy. But in all that time no one had ever
hinted to me that I could observe myself in this meditative way, or that
by developing certain faculties of my mind I could see into my deepest
biological and psychological conditioning for myself, and in the process
even unravel a few threads of it.

Although psychotherapy had given me a glimpse into the influences of my personal history on my present life, I had never explored
the much more powerful impact of life itself, or how just being a human
or an animal has laid down the basic conditions of my existence. I had
never learned to understand or to *feel* myself as part of nature in any
way, or as interwoven with the world in any form. While psychotherapy

1

had shown me how to see into the origins of my personality, I had been given no clue how to see through it; I had been taught how to gain some freedom for myself, but never how to gain freedom *from* myself.

As it is for many people, my first meditation retreat was therefore full of fascinating, painful, self-shattering revelations. I was amazed to discover a pure knowing part of my mind that was somewhat different from my thinking mind. I had never imagined that I could actually listen to myself think, nor that it would be so humbling to do so.

Our culture emphasizes the development of intellect—reading, writing, and 'rithmatic—and I had come to place the highest value on thinking and my ability to manipulate thoughts. After all, that is what we are graded on in school. Like most of us, I came to regard what was in my mind as my primary identity. In some strange sense, who "I" was did not involve the earth, the history of life, the cosmos, hardly even my own body. What I had grown up believing, quite literally, is that "I think, therefore I am." Perhaps it would be more accurate to say, "I think therefore I think I am."

During my first few meditation retreats, I was quite surprised to hear myself thinking *against my will*. I would be trying to pay single-minded attention to my breath, and my mind would continue to produce all sorts of thoughts and ideas. Who was doing this thinking? And if I am not the director of my thinking, then what am I doing with all that free time? More to the point, if I am not my thinking, who am I?

The practice of mindfulness meditation has allowed me to look clearly and sometimes even calmly at my mind and body, and to ask questions like these. After many years of meditation and study I don't claim any great final liberation, but I do feel that my primary identity has shifted. More and more I feel myself included in the world and, just as important, the world included in me.

Sometimes I think it strange that I perhaps wouldn't have felt this inclusion—or for that matter known of this method of self-observation—all on my own. The attitude of meditative mindfulness seems so obvious to me now, and the practice seems so necessary to a clear understanding of my life. Shouldn't we all just discover these things as a natural part of our human development?

Over the years, as I continued to study Buddhist ideas and practices, I began to notice an amazing correspondence between this ancient wisdom tradition and the discoveries of modern science. What first captured my interest, along with that of many others, were the breakthroughs in the fields of quantum physics and astronomy that seemed to corroborate ancient Buddhist perspectives. By the late seventies, however, I had become equally fascinated with the stories coming from the natural sciences, especially from the fields of evolutionary biology and psychology. These disciplines had begun revealing in very precise detail how deeply embedded and interwoven humans are with all of life and nature, echoing the most fundamental of Buddhist insights.

The more I studied both Buddhism and the evolutionary sciences, the more they seemed to me to be a marriage made—let's say—in evolution. The two disciplines draw strikingly similar maps of mental and emotional life, and also agree on the fundamental laws of nature and living systems. Most importantly, I am convinced that Buddhism and evolutionary science can serve each other in ways that have profound implications for all of us.

As I will explain in detail throughout this book, the evolutionary sciences lend support and guidance to the Buddhist practices of self-liberation, offering very specific information about our place in the scheme of things. The sciences show us how interwoven we are with all life through the history of molecules, cells, bones, and brains.

Buddhist meditation, in turn, can make the latest discoveries of evolutionary science relevant and vital in our lives. Through Buddhist practices, the scientific revolution can actually be placed in the service of the spiritual. Together the two can offer us what I call *evolutionary wisdom*.

This wisdom is quite simply the deep realization of our nature *as* nature. I am not just referring to an abstract knowledge of other primate species as our ancestors, but rather to a deep sense of our co-emergence with the elements, the sea and atmosphere, cellular life and sunlight, plants and animals, sentience—the whole evolutionary she-bang. Evolutionary wisdom is also a recognition and exploration of the special gifts we seem to have been given by nature, and how we might use them to enhance our human condition and the life of this planet.

It is important to state that this book is not about getting rid of our personality or individuality—as if that were even possible—but rather about gaining access to our most basic identity. When we can experience ourselves as part of the processes of biological and cosmic evolution, we automatically begin to break free from the domination of ego. We are finally able to loosen the tight shoe of self. Our lives gain new dimension, context, gestalt. We begin to give ourselves some space.

❧

Being Nature is a practical guide, offering meditations and reflective exercises that I hope will lead you to greater self-awareness, and thereby to increased freedom and happiness. Most of the exercises in the book are variations of traditional Buddhist practices, interpreted for our time through the filters of modern science and intended to be provocative, easy, and even fun to do.

These ideas and practices come, for the most part, from the Theravada school of Buddhism, known as the Path of the Elders. This school is based on the earliest written record of the Buddha's teaching, compiled five hundred years after his death in numerous texts collectively called the Pali Canon. The most significant segments of the Pali Canon are the discourses (*sutras,* in Sanskrit) given by the Buddha as he instructed his followers on the path of self-awareness and liberation.

The Path of the Elders has been preserved in India, Myanmar, Thailand, and Sri Lanka, and it has become one of the most popular Buddhist schools in the modern Western world. The primary meditation practices of the Elders' tradition are often referred to as "insight" (*vipassana*), and most of them are based on the development of the mental faculty known as mindfulness.

For scientific advice, I have drawn from writings and interviews with experts and interpreters from many disciplines, but especially from those in neuroscience, evolutionary biology, and psychology. In particular, I have been inspired by people engaged in some way with both science and meditation practice who have brought the two together in their work, including Jon Kabat-Zinn, Daniel Goleman, Mark Epstein, Francisco Varela, Candace Pert, Rick Hanson, and Fritjof Capra, among others.

This book is dedicated to the perennial teachings of Buddhism, which are to foster self-awareness and compassion, and to relieve suffering—in short, to evolve. As Buddhist scholar Robert A. F. Thurman has said, "Buddhism is an evolutionary sport." This book is an invitation to play that game, and to the increase of wisdom, peace, and happiness that it can offer.

PART ONE

To Study the Self

꙳ ꙳

CHAPTER ONE

A Case of
Mistaken Identity

True happiness consists in eliminating the false idea of "I."

THE BUDDHA

The true value of a human being is determined primarily
by the measure and the sense in which he has attained
liberation from the self.

ALBERT EINSTEIN

According to the world's great spiritual traditions and perennial philosophies, the critical question that each of us must ask ourselves is "Who am I?" Our response is of vital importance to our happiness and well-being. How at ease we feel in our body, mind, and in the world, as well as how we behave toward others and the environment all revolve around how we come to view ourselves in the larger scheme of things.

If you were asked to describe yourself, how would you respond? Most people might say their name, occupation, family status, age, gender, nationality, ethnic background, and religious affiliation. Only after further probing will some people add that they are *alive,* or that they are a human, conscious, an animal, a vertebrate, a biped, a primate, or an earthling. The most essential aspects of our existence—and the ones we hold most in common with others—are often afterthoughts or completely missing from how we see ourselves.

In our time, many of us seem to be increasingly lost in our *personal* dramas. Spiritually and psychologically we live inside a bubble of self, as though we are "in here" and the rest of the world is "out there." From moment to moment we believe that we are acting "on" the world, rarely noticing that we are "of" the world. Our social and economic philosophy says, "you are on your own," and even our religions tell us that salvation is an individual matter between each of us and our god. On all sides, we sense ourselves isolated and apart from the rest of creation.

Perhaps strangest of all, we experience our human life and society as different from nature, somehow detached from universal laws and the unfolding of biological evolution. This feeling of separateness continues in spite of the fact that our sciences have shown us the specific ways in which we have been fashioned out of other life forms and shaped by natural forces. Most of us do not carry any sense of being created in that way or as being part of those processes.

Our feeling of separation from nature is apparent in our language. For instance, when an earthquake or flood occurs we talk of a "natural disaster," but we don't consider our wars or economic upheavals as natural disasters—as if nature has nothing whatsoever to do with the way *we* behave. In the service of survival, our species was given the ability to see ourselves as separate from the world as a smart adaptation.

The idea that we are separate and autonomous beings is not only mistaken but is a fundamental source of our suffering. When we don't feel a part of some grander design we are forced to carry all of the meaning of life on our own shoulders. We must judge our worth according to purely personal goals or else in comparison with others, fostering feelings of loneliness, competition, and fear. Without any sense of being governed by universal laws and processes, we almost inevitably end up blaming ourselves for not finding enough happiness or security, or else blaming others. When we don't feel part of life or the world we also lose a sense of wonder and can easily become cynical or sad. These are all symptoms of the metaphysical malaise of individualism, the disease we suffer from today.

> *We don't have to think of ourselves as isolated, interior monads—that is not the unalterable truth about ourselves; it is just one perspective on ourselves, and perspectives can change.*
>
> PHILIP CUSHMAN, *CONSTRUCTING AMERICA, CONSTRUCTING THE SELF*

Why did we pry ourselves loose from earth and sky and other creatures and wander off alone? Evolution made us do it. What led to human supremacy on this planet is precisely our ability to find differences, to make distinctions. As a result, we became good at breaking the world into pieces (in our minds, as well), and then moving those pieces around to suit our perceived needs and desires. The bargain, however, was Faustian. The dividing intellect that gave us power over things also severed the primal umbilical cord; it cut us off from the rest of creation.

According to the Bible we were once integrated with the natural world but were banished from that "garden" when Adam and Eve ate from the Tree of the Knowledge of Good and Evil. Perhaps we call that mythical moment "the fall" because we consider it the beginning of our feelings of separation.

It was not into sin that we fell, for that implies that we knew what we were doing. The fall was a banishment from the grace of union. We fell out of the garden of oneness. Biting into the apple brought us self-consciousness, and that led to a new kind of suffering in the world—the individual, personal kind.

Our feelings of separateness and individuality seem to have increased over the course of human history. As we study the past, we realize that it didn't always feel this way to be somebody: the boundaries of self were not always so clearly drawn. As philosopher Charles Taylor writes in his widely acclaimed book *Sources of the Self,* "Talk about 'identity' in the modern sense would have been incomprehensible to our forebears of a couple of centuries ago." It seems safe to say that prior to just the last century or so, virtually nobody held the opinion that you can be anyone you want to be in this lifetime.

The concept of self—along with the innermost sense of what it feels like to be a person—changes over time. A nomadic tribesman of 500 BCE, a medieval peasant, and a modern middle-class corporate employee would have very different notions about their place in the cosmos, their self-importance, their personal freedom, and their relationship to the forces of nature and other people. Who we think we are depends to a significant degree upon which wave we ride in the streams of biological and cultural evolution; where and when we are born. We don't create our self so much as the evolving idea of "self" creates us.

Not so very long ago in biological time, people did not necessarily believe that they were in charge of their lives or, for that matter, even their own minds. In his now famous study *The Origin of Consciousness in the Breakdown of the Bi-Cameral Mind,* Julian Jaynes claims that in early Greek culture "the gods take the place of consciousness." Jaynes cites passages from the *Iliad* that indicate that the Greeks who lived around 1000 BCE had "no will of their own and certainly no notion of free will." According to Jaynes, the early Greeks heard their thought process as voices of the gods, an interpretation that today we might call schizophrenic.

Approximately five hundred years later, just as Gautama Buddha was declaring a doctrine of "non-self" in Asia, a radically new "self" emerged in the Hellenic world. Socrates, Plato, and Aristotle heralded the apparent power of each individual to manipulate the contents of his or her own mind. It was no longer the gods' voices that were heard inside the heads of people, but their own. The assumption that each person can think and reason for themselves marked a major shift in human consciousness, as well as in the sense of personal identity.

An entirely new degree of individuality seemed to emerge in Europe during the Enlightenment. Individuals grew more and more identified with their own mind, which was seen as the source and center of the personal self. The thinkers of the era became so enamored of their powers of intellect and invention that they declared the mind and its "self" to be superior to and independent of the world of matter and nature. Power was taken away from God and truth from the church, and both were given over to human reason and science. In theory at least, the individual was freed from any outside authority or conditions. Ironically, just as the Enlightenment's science was proving that the Earth was not the center of the universe, its philosophers were granting that exalted place to each individual.

The self that pervades the modern world is completely convinced of its own autonomy and separateness. Over time we have developed what psychological historian Philip Cushman calls "the bounded, masterful self," an individual who believes that he or she is completely independent of outside forces. This modern self lives in a "culture of narcissism," with very little sense of being part of either a grand cosmic design, the unfolding processes of nature, or even a communal or historical destiny. In the mirror of our culture and in the mirror of our private bathrooms we see only the individual. Upon closer examination, this image begins to look like a hallucination: we seem to be suffering from a new form of schizophrenia in which we label *all* of the different voices in our heads as "I" or "mine." Believing them all to be ours is as far-fetched as believing they all belong to the gods.

Human beings have reached what may well be a pivotal
stage in their evolution. They have been created by the

universe, in the universe, as an integral part of the universe. They have passed through a difficult period when their strong day-to-day experience of selfhood and their cultural conditioning have made them feel detached from the reality in which they are permanently embedded. And now they are beginning to see beyond the self again into the truth of their condition.

DAVID DARLING, *ZEN PHYSICS*

Now we have come full circle, at least in our knowledge of ourselves. Perhaps the human mind has finally become masterful enough to see through its own hubris and is now bringing us to a more balanced and satisfying understanding of who we are in the world. Ironically, the dividing intellect—in its incarnation as modern science—is showing us our oneness with all things. The physicists have found evidence that we are subatomically joined at the hip to absolutely everything else in creation. The chemists and biologists have named the common molecules that make us coexistent with the atmosphere, the earth, and all other living things. The geneticists have unraveled molecular codes revealing that microbes, salamanders, horseshoe crabs, apes, and humans all share common ancestry. The evolutionary scientists tell us a story of our emergence from a long lineage of beings in what seems like a miraculous process of bubbling, twitching, struggling life, re-creating itself as it interactively adjusts to the ever-changing conditions of Earth ecology.

But still, if a bunch of esteemed scientists got you in a room and told you of their discoveries, you might say, "Sure, I know all that." And then you would stand up and walk away, continuing to believe in your own independent, self-created self. There "you" go, again.

If we could only evolve into our new scientific understanding, if we could somehow integrate our knowledge of interconnection and let it infuse our lives—that would mark a revolution in both consciousness and behavior. If we could experience our existence as part of the wondrous processes of biological and cosmic evolution, our lives would gain new meaning and joy. The mystics have been making this point for centuries. As Alan Watts wrote, "We do not need a new religion or a new bible. We need a new experience—a new feeling of what it is to be 'I.'"

THE BUDDHA'S LOOK INSIDE

Within the Buddhist tradition there exist powerful, time-tested, and accessible methods for healing our perceived separation from the world around us. The techniques of Buddhist insight meditation were specifically designed as ways to explore and experience the natural forces working through us at every moment. These meditations and reflections are meant to liberate us from the suffocation of a mistaken separate identity.

In particular, as I will explain in detail later in the book, the Buddhist meditation series known as the Four Foundations of Mindfulness can be understood and practiced as an evolutionary journey. These exercises guide us through our body, emotions, and mind, and in the process reveal our nature as nature. Although evolutionary scientists are uncovering this same truth, there is a crucial difference in their process, and that is in the direction of their gaze. Scientists investigate life by looking outside of themselves, while Buddhist meditators look inward. In either direction reality displays roughly the same qualities: scientists and meditators give uncannily similar accounts of everything from brain functions to subatomic realities. As inside, so outside. The big difference is that by holding these truths inside ourselves the information becomes *personal*. Experiencing the laws of nature working within us begins to alter our sense of who we are and how we feel about our life.

The methods of science do not necessarily have this effect. Physicists can understand subatomic reality in the outside world and forget that it is going on inside of them. A neuroscientist can study someone else's brain functions and remark on the absence of a director or "self," while still convinced that a self—maybe even one deserving of the Pulitzer Prize—is conducting the study. Evolutionary psychologists can trace the primal origins of many human behaviors, and continue to believe, as they groom themselves in the mirror every morning, that they are the sole authors of their own.

It seems that knowledge of the external world alone isn't enough to transform us. We have all seen the Earth from the moon or from outer space, and yet, in spite of optimistic predictions, that image does not seem to have significantly altered our sense of ourselves or our place in the cosmos. What is becoming clear is that the habits of the heart are too deeply entrenched to be uprooted by abstract knowledge or even by a single image, no matter how powerful. Paradigms are heavy, and it takes a lot of force to shift them even a fraction.

As meditators go inside to explore and experience the nature of their bodies and minds, the insights slowly begin to seep into the marrow of their being, resetting what the neuroscientists call "resonating neuronal assemblies." What is discovered and perceived is finally "realized," a word used by many spiritual traditions to mean that one is starting to live and experience life according to their own deepest understanding.

LANDING ON EARTH

I suggest that once you become aware of the idea of evolution, once you begin to feel that things do change through time, then your perception of everything around you is enhanced. Another dimension is added to your view of the world, and that is the fourth dimension: time. You begin to perceive that an animal or a plant and the lineage to which it belongs, and the planet itself, are like a flame; not so much a thing as a performance, always becoming something else; and that each of us and our species as a whole are part of the overall unfolding.

COLIN TUDGE, *THE TIME BEFORE HISTORY*

The aim of all great spiritual traditions is to offer us relief from the dramas of self and history, to remind us that we are part of much grander projects than these. In that sense, I suggest that experiencing ourselves as part of biological evolution can be understood as a complete spiritual path. The fantastic story of evolving life and consciousness contains as many miracles as any bible and as much majesty as any pantheon of divinities. The drama of Earth life's creative expression and the puzzle of where it might be leading can fill us with enough suspense and wonder to last at least a lifetime. And the idea that we are part of its unfolding can offer us meaning and purpose. Equally important, the difficulties, pain, and death inherent in all life can teach us about the fundamental conditions of our own. And if the spiritual has something to do with humility, then the scale of nature, from the uncountable number of cells in our brain to the Grand Canyon to the vast numbers of galaxy clusters just now being discovered will certainly serve the purpose.

To know ourselves as emerging from earth life doesn't in any way deny our divinity: it only seems to deny our *exclusive* divinity. The sacred is alive not just in us, but everywhere. Nature can even serve as the text of our religion: the holy can be seen inscribed in the veins of the leaves and in the vessels of our blood. Nature is the medium that nurtured our consciousness as well as our imagination, and therefore is the mother of all our realities, even the realm of the gods.

If spiritual *liberation* means feeling part of something greater than oneself, then, as Buddhist philosopher and ecologist Joanna Macy proposes, "Rather than being liberated *from* life, we can be liberated *into* life." A nature-based spirituality would foster the realization that what defines our individual human life is, first and foremost, life. Secondarily it is human, and only thirdly is it individual.

As we navigate through this still-young millennium, facing increasing news of ecological catastrophe, many people are searching for ways to "reconnect" with natural processes, or, more accurately, to realize their innate connection. The Buddhist practices of self-awareness, supported by the knowledge of evolutionary science, can help us gain a sense of what Vietnamese Zen master Thich Nhat Hanh calls our "interbeing." These practices can help us ground the great mystery and, in the process, make ourselves feel at home again.

> *Molecules awoke one morning to find that atoms were inside them, enfolded in their very being. Cells awoke one morning to find that molecules were actually inside them, as part of their being. And you might awake one morning and find that nature is a part of you, literally internal to your being. You would then treat nature as you would your lungs or kidneys. A spontaneous environmental ethics surges forth from your heart, and you will never again look at a river, a leaf, a deer, a robin, in the same way.*
>
> KEN WILBER, *A BRIEF HISTORY OF EVERYTHING*

❧❧ ❦❦

CHAPTER TWO

The Buddha
Was a Biologist

It is our contention that . . . Asian philosophy, particularly of the Buddhist tradition, is a second renaissance in the cultural history of the West, with the potential to be equally important as the discovery of Greek thought in the European renaissance. [Asian philosophy] never became a purely abstract occupation. It was tied to specific disciplined methods for knowing—different methods of meditation.

FRANCISCO VARELA,
THE EMBODIED MIND

Buddhist meditation practices and scientific exploration reveal two ways of knowing. With the scientific method, we look outside of ourselves for truth, dividing up the world to see if reality's secrets are hiding in the cracks. Meanwhile, with meditation, we direct our attention inward, relying on experiential knowing, seeking to resolve the questions themselves in the realization of non-duality and the great mystery of consciousness.

As they compare notes, scientists and Buddhist scholars alike have been astounded by the fact that the two ways of knowing have arrived at so many similar conclusions. Physics is one arena where the two have found agreement. As impossible as it must seem to physicists who use sophisticated bubble chambers and laser photography to study subatomic events, Buddhists have uncovered at least the basic principles of subatomic physics through their meditation practices. Meditation can reveal that there is no solidity anywhere, that the observer cannot be separated from what is observed, that phenomena seem to appear out of emptiness, and that everything affects everything else in a co-emergent system that scientists have acknowledged and named "nonlocality." These insights have been discovered by many meditators who have simply focused their attention inward.

The Buddhist and scientific maps of mind and cognition are strikingly similar. Furthermore, the Buddhists have for centuries been studying the elusive nature of "self" and consciousness, concepts that continue to befuddle the neuroscientists. Many Buddhists have even resolved these puzzles, at least to the individual meditator's satisfaction.

Buddhist meditation itself could be understood as a form of scientific research. Meditators try to maintain the scientific attitude of objectivity while investigating themselves. They too want to look at life without prejudicing the study with personal desires or preset theories. "Just the facts, ma'am."

A scientist might argue that his findings are objective because they can be verified by someone replicating the experiments or redoing the mathematical equations. However, every Buddhist meditator who undertakes a specific path of inquiry is, in a sense, redoing the experiment, and most will arrive at similar conclusions about the nature of self and reality. In mindfulness meditation, what is known as "the progress of insight" unfolds in a relatively standard fashion for most people. The Buddha wants each of us to become a scientist, using ourselves as subjects. He recommends a careful deconstruction of the seemingly solid realities of mind and body as a way to explore their sources, and thus reveal our oneness with the world. As it says in the *Abhidhamma,* an early Buddhist text, "the first task of insight (*vipassana*) meditation is . . . the dissecting of an apparently compact mass."

Modern science also set about the task of disassembling reality and has found—miracle of miracles—that oneness is right there, in reality's very core. If it has proven anything, scientific research over the past few decades has validated the mystical vision as *the* ultimate truth. Nothing can be separated from anything else. The scientists attempt to express this oneness by inserting the connector: wave-particle, space-time, matter-energy.

Although modern science has helped humanity achieve new levels of material comfort, its greatest gift may yet turn out to be spiritual—a more accurate and satisfying way of understanding ourselves. Instead of reducing humans to material processes, as some critics assert, scientists are simply showing us the specific threads that connect us to all of life and the universe.

> *A single protein molecule or a single finger print, a single syllable on the radio or a single idea of yours implies the whole historical reach of stellar and organic evolution. It is enough to make you tingle all the time.*
>
> JOHN PLATT,
> THE STEPS TO MAN

The Buddha was a great scientist of the self. It is clear in the Pāli Canon that he was not much concerned with cosmic consciousness, and there is no evidence that he believed in any god or goddess. He was also silent on the question of a first cause, saying it would be impossible to trace the "karma," the complete history of either an individual or the universe. Instead, throughout his discourses we find the Buddha emphasizing what I would call "biological consciousness."

The Buddha's meditation instructions in the Pāli Canon are almost exclusively focused on the natural processes of our physical and mental life. He tells us to meditate on our skin and bones, our nervous system, the processes of walking, hearing, seeing, and thinking. According to the Buddha, everything we need to know about life and reality can be found inside "this fathom-long body."

Throughout his teachings, for instance, the Buddha emphasizes the impermanent nature of all phenomena. Remembering this universal truth (documented from Heraclitus to Heisenberg) is critical to our personal happiness, because the fact that everything is in transition means that we can't hold on to any object or experience, nor to life itself. If we forget about impermanence and try to grasp or hold on to things, we will inevitably create suffering for ourselves.

The Buddha tells us to become personally familiar with this truth by meditating on the changes that take place inside of us at every moment:

> *Herein a person contemplates as impermanent and not as permanent, the pleasant, unpleasant and neutral feelings . . . the feelings born of visual impressions, sound-impressions, smell-impressions; (etc.) . . . the corporeal phenomena . . . water, heat, skin, flesh, blood, sinews, bone marrow, (etc.) . . . visual consciousness, auditory consciousness, olfactory consciousness, (etc.). . . . Contemplating them [all] as impermanent, the meditator abandons the notion of permanency . . . [and] by relinquishing, the meditator abandons craving.*
>
> SATIPATTHANA-KATHA

According to the Buddha, by experiencing our own impermanent nature—by feeling it and reflecting upon it regularly—we can learn to inhabit this truth and live by it. As we grow familiar with the radical impermanence of every moment's experience, we may no longer get so lost in our own desire system; we don't hold on as tightly or get so "hung up." We are able to live more in harmony with the way things are. This is one example of how the Buddha was able to use his scientific insights in the service of spirituality.

> *Those who drink of the deepest truths live happily with a serene mind.*
>
> DHAMMAPADA

As a spiritual biologist, the Buddha studied the human condition thoroughly. He gave a broad outline of his findings in the Four Noble Truths, the first of which announces that life is inherently unsatisfactory, a time of continual neediness and desire accompanied by some measure of pain, sadness, sickness, and inevitable old age and death. The First Noble Truth (*dukkha* in Pali, translated as "suffering") is part of the deal when we get a human body and nervous system—period. Critics cite the First Noble Truth as proof that the Buddha was negative about life, but he was simply making a scientific observation.

This human condition may seem inhumane to us, but that only means that it doesn't meet our standards of fairness. We would like life to be different, and ironically, that desire itself can become a major source of our suffering.

All of this isn't to deny that there is joy, love, pleasure, and fun in a life, but the hard facts are much more certain. It simply is not easy having a body, fighting gravity from morning to night, being forever in need of food, warmth, and shelter, and driven by the urge to procreate. These are the biological conditions we are born into, and what the Buddha saw was that we need to come to a deep inner understanding and acceptance of them if we are ever to find any peace of mind or ease in life. Indeed, meditators often report feelings of great relief when they begin to acknowledge the First Noble Truth—and that it does apply to them.

The Buddha's Second Noble Truth (*samudaya* in Pali, translated as "arising") attributes the arising of human suffering to the fact that we live in an almost constant state of desire. According to the Buddha, we are born into this condition as well: It is part of our evolutionary inheritance, the karma of taking form. He explains in detail how simply having a body and senses and coming into contact with the world will create pleasant or unpleasant sensations that will automatically lead to reactions of desire or aversion. This process is instinctual, a function of our nervous system, which operates according to the biological law of stimulus-response. The Buddha saw that this organic condition keeps us continually dissatisfied and off-balance.

With great psychological insight, the Buddha recognized that our desires fall into three categories. One he called the "desire for existence," which we might think of as the survival instinct, which gets translated into building strong walls around our houses, opening a savings account, finding good doctors, or even seeking a religion that will promise the ultimate security of everlasting life. The Buddha also saw a complementary desire within us for "nonexistence," which can be translated into the urge to lose oneself in sex, food, movies, or adventure, or by some means to "get out" of oneself. Even the mystical search can be seen as a desire for nonexistence, a wish to dissolve once again into the amniotic fluids or the oceanic Oneness. The Buddha's last category of desire is for sense pleasure, perhaps the easiest to notice. It's the pleasure principle, present in almost everything we do.

I am always startled when I watch my mind for any length of time in meditation, just to discover that these three desire gears are all there, going around independently, with an ever-changing array of objects attached to them. Desire is perfectly natural, I discover, but it has less to do with "me" than I ever could imagine.

Like most people, I usually believe that I suffer only because the desire of this moment remains unfulfilled, until, perhaps in meditation, I recognize that I am caught on a treadmill. When my mind grows quiet, I am able to see that desire itself is what keeps me dissatisfied. This is difficult to notice, precisely because so few moments of our life are without desire. Meditation can offer an experience of another possibility.

> *There is nothing more important to true growth than realizing that you are not the voice of the mind—you are the one who hears it.*
>
> MICHAEL A. SINGER,
> *THE UNTETHERED SOUL*

The Buddha's Third Noble Truth (*nirodha* in Pali, translated as "cessation") is his most significant biological insight, that nature has given us the ability to train our minds to bring us new levels to end suffering and attain freedom and satisfaction. During his own awakening, the Buddha realized that as humans we are able to see into our primal reactivity and in the process learn how to gain some freedom from it. Evolution has gifted us with the potential for new degrees of self-awareness, and perhaps even the ability, on some level, to take part in our own evolution. If we learn how to develop this potential, we might yet live up to our self-applied labels of "conscious," or *Homo sapiens sapiens,* the twice-knowing human. We may even be able to find a way to become a more contented species. "I teach one thing and one thing only," said the Buddha: "suffering, and the end of suffering."

The Buddha's Fourth Noble Truth (*magga* in Pali, translated as "path") is the most important one of all, because it tells us *how* to end our suffering. In this fourth and final truth the Buddha explains how to live a life that does not cause harm to others, partially so that the mind, undisturbed by remorse, guilt, or anger, remains open to the task of self-investigation. The Buddha then gives the basic instructions for developing the vital skills of concentration and mindfulness and explains how to apply these in meditation in order to realize our true nature. This is the Path Leading to the Cessation of Suffering.

PART TWO

The Gift of Mindfulness

CHAPTER THREE

~~>> <<~~

Mindfulness

The Opposable Thumb
of Consciousness

To better understand our human condition and learn how to develop its potential as outlined in the Four Noble Truths, we begin by investigating ourselves closely. We become archeologists and dig deep beneath the surface into the most basic aspects of our being. For this task we need a sharp tool to dig with, a clear eye to see with, and an attitude of impartial curiosity. These are all provided by the mental faculty known in Buddhism as mindfulness.

Mindfulness is perhaps best described as "a non-interfering, non-reactive awareness." It is *pure knowing,* without any of the projections of our ego or personality added to the knowing.

Every human being can become mindful—it is a gift of evolution—although most people are not aware that they possess this power. It is as if there were an opposable thumb, hanging limply in our mind's tool kit, waiting to be exercised and articulated so that it can touch and hold reality in a completely different way.

Although mindfulness is not something you have to create, before you can use it you have to learn what this mental gear feels like, and then learn how to shift into it. Actually, mindfulness is more a way of shifting out of gear into neutral—disengaging the drive shaft of your personality, putting your survival brain or reactive self in idle.

During meditation we shift into mindfulness by developing a less reactive relationship with whatever appears in our field of awareness. For instance, if we notice that a thought has arisen, we simply acknowledge that fact, without automatically analyzing the thought or judging it good or bad. In ordinary consciousness, we would engage in some way with the thought, get involved in its meaning or emotional charge, and lose the ability to see the nature of the thought as a thought. We might fail to notice its origin, context, effect, and duration. Instead, we become the thought. Who we are collapses into this passing event, and we become completely identified with its content. Likewise with sounds, sights, sensations, smells, or emotions. In our so-called "normal" state of consciousness we are therefore continually lost in the drama of our lives, unaware of how the process that creates our reality is taking place.

One way to explain how mindfulness works is through the analogy of the movie theater. When we are watching the screen, we are absorbed in the momentum of the story, our thoughts and emotions manipulated by the images we are seeing. But if just for a moment we were to turn around and look toward the back of the theater at the projector, we would see how these images are being produced. We would recognize that what we are lost in is nothing more than flickering beams of light. Although we might be able to turn back and lose ourselves once again in the movie, its power over us would be diminished. The illusion-maker has been seen.

Similarly, in mindfulness meditation, we look deeply into our own movie-making process. We see the mechanics of how our personal story gets created, and how we project that story onto everything we see, hear, taste, smell, think, and do.

Of course, seeing through your own drama sounds terribly unromantic, but that is precisely the point. Mindfulness meditation can provide an antidote to sentimentality. When we see how our personal picture show is created, we no longer have to take the movie quite so personally, and that means the potential for a lot less suffering.

Because we are normally lost in the contents of our mind, we also fail to notice what is called in Buddhism "the true nature of mind." We don't recognize the mind's original clarity and openness or experience the wonder and ease that come from that recognition. Strangely enough, we don't realize this true nature of mind because each of us is standing in the line of sight. With the magic lever of mindfulness we can pull aside the screen of personality and see for ourselves.

Although mindfulness is available to us in any situation, its investigative power can be tapped potently in silent meditation. When mindfulness is sharply focused and refined, it can give us a penetrating look into the nature of self and reality. It becomes the fundamental tool of evolutionary wisdom.

One important aspect of mindfulness when applied in meditation is the attitude of "choiceless awareness." When we meditate we simply turn on the light of our awareness without any preference for what appears (except in special guided meditations or reflections). We are not looking for anything in particular, nor are we trying to create any kind of experience.

Choiceless awareness allows the meditator to see how our experience creates itself; how sense impressions, thoughts, and feelings arise without our willing them; how they interact and influence each other. By engaging the quality of choiceless awareness, we can extract ourselves from the contents of *what* we think and feel and start to explore *how* we think and feel.

To understand choiceless awareness, just imagine that you are a naturalist walking through a forest. Your task is simply to investigate and take note of what is there: "pine tree, bear scat, lichen, field mouse, sound of creek," et cetera. You are not trying to find anything in particular, but you are extremely interested in what naturally grows in the forest, how one thing influences another, and how it all coexists.

Just so, choiceless awareness can help us focus on what is appearing inside our own mind and body: planning thought, twitching sensation, the sound of a distant automobile being heard. We enter the wilderness of our "own" world, but only as an observer. Chances are we will find some thickets, a few wild animals, storms of various types, and a lot of bugs.

> *All things can be mastered by mindfulness.*
> THE BUDDHA, *ANGUTTARA NIKAYA*

Some Hindu yogis may have employed mindfulness before he did, but it is Gautama, the Buddha, who must be given credit for raising this faculty of mind to its highest power. The Buddha recognized that a nonreactive consciousness was essential to his own awakening, and he made it the fulcrum upon which all of his meditation practices are based. His greatest gift to humanity was to develop a systematic way for anyone to discover and cultivate their own mindfulness, no matter who they are.

One reason more people were not familiar with mindfulness until fairly recently was because the skill was cloistered, practiced primarily by esoteric branches of religious traditions, most notably in Asia. Even there, mindfulness practices were most often cultivated by those drawn to monasteries and meditation centers.

In the last decade or so, mindfulness has exploded in popularity throughout the modern secular world. Lately it seems to be everywhere. It's being taught to healthcare workers, educators, business executives, professional athletes, and school children. It's used for better concentration, stress reduction, and pain management. Mindfulness is all over the media—even gracing the cover of *Time* magazine.

As mindfulness spreads into many corners of our culture, it would be unfortunate to forget the original and most significant use of this power of mind—as the key to self-awareness and spiritual liberation. As the noted twentieth-century Buddhist monk and scholar Nyanaponika Thera wrote about mindfulness, in *The Heart of Buddhist Meditation:*

> [It] recovers for [us] the lost pearl of our freedom, snatching it from the jaws of the dragon Time. . . . Mindfulness cuts [us] loose from the fetters of the past . . . and stops [us] from chaining [ourselves] even now . . . to anticipated events of the future. Right Mindfulness restores to [us] a freedom that is to be found only in the present.

The Buddha knew that he could not anoint us with self-awareness or liberation, but that it had to be found by each person within themselves. What he did give us was a precise method for using mindfulness to examine our true nature—the very method he had used to realize his own enlightenment.

The Buddha's guide to self-exploration is contained in one of the most important texts in all of Buddhism—the *Mahasatipatthana Sutra,* the great (*maha*) discourse (*sutra*) on the establishment of mindfulness (*satipattana*). This sutra is especially revered in the Buddhist countries of Southeast Asia, and while it may not be as dazzling as the enigmatic Heart Sutra of Zen or *The Tibetan Book of the Dead,* for many of us, it is perhaps the most straightforward and practical guide to awakening of them all.

Although the *Mahasatipatthana Sutra* is only about ten thousand words long, it sets forth the basic tenets of the Buddha's teaching and provides the basis for literally hundreds of different meditation practices and reflections. The *Mahasatipatthana Sutra* is the cornerstone of insight meditation.

The meditations and reflections described in the sutra do not require a belief in Buddha, nirvana, reincarnation, or any other concept or deity. They are not esoteric, do not concern themselves with cosmic reality, and do not promise any sudden, bolt-of-enlightening realizations. On this path no divine grace can be expected from a guru or god, and none is necessary. The *Mahasatipatthana Sutra* describes a clearly marked, systematic, down-to-earth process of self-realization that everyone can follow for themselves. It is a text of practical mysticism.

> *This is the way for the purification of beings, for the overcoming of sorrow and lamentation, for the destroying of pain and grief, for reaching the right path, for the realization of Nirvana, namely the four Foundations of Mindfulness.*
>
> MAHASATIPATTHANA SUTRA

The series of meditation exercises described in the *Mahasatipatthana Sutra* are called the Four Foundations of Mindfulness. These four are the fundamental components of the human condition: the physical elements that make up our body, including the process of breathing; the nervous system that gives us sentience; the emotional life and psychic states that color our experience; and the ideas, concepts, beliefs, and consciousness that together we call the mind. In the sutra, the Buddha guides us through these Four Foundations, showing us the basic aspects of our being through the special lens of mindfulness.

The meditations on the Four Foundations, as timeless as the human condition, seem especially appropriate for the modern age. They offer us a way to experience our existence, not as an isolated monad, but as an integrated part of universal cycles and processes. They are deep-ecology practices, ways of exploring our nature *as nature*. These exercises can establish us in our connection with each other, and with all other forms of life on earth.

CHAPTER FOUR

≫≫ ⧨⧨

The First Foundation
of Mindfulness

The Body and Breath

There is one thing that, when cultivated and regularly practiced, leads to deep spiritual intention, to peace, to mindfulness and clear comprehension, to vision and knowledge, to a happy life here and now, and to the culmination of wisdom and awakening. And what is that one thing? It is mindfulness centered on the body.

THE BUDDHA, *ANGUTTARA NIKAYA*

The Buddha understood that if we are going to experience the roots of our identity, we need to start with the most elemental aspect of our being—the body. In the *Mahasatipatthana Sutra,* he begins the sequence of meditations with the instructions: "Having gone into the forest, or to the root of a tree, or to an empty place" one should "abide contemplating the body as body both internally and externally." Exploring the nature of our physical existence is the Buddha's First Foundation of Mindfulness, and the beginning of our practice of evolutionary wisdom.

Contemplating "the body as body" does not mean contemplating "my" body. In another teaching text, the *Samyutta Nikaya,* the Buddha says, "This body does not belong to you or to anyone else. It is the result of previous activity, and for now, it should be felt." The Buddha is explaining that this body is not of our creation nor choosing but arises out of a long process of multiple causes and conditions, what today we might call evolutionary adaptation.

The Buddha is telling us to dive into the body and feel it, to become intimate with it from head to toe and inside out. Through that exploration we will come to know the body as an organic process; as coexistent with the elements of nature and all of earthlife. We will realize that "my body" is not really mine. It's a loaner. It is evolution's body.

Come to think of it, I don't remember ordering the body I got. No catalogue of choices was offered.

Sometimes, while meditating on the body, I can feel the fact that I am, indeed, a medium-sized mammal. I am also a vertebrate. And so are you. To experience this for yourself, just grind your teeth together for a few seconds and feel the shape of your skull. We humans share a bone structure with all the chewers on the planet—we have hinged jaws and teeth. Our skeleton has been formed by five hundred million years of continual adaptations, and its bony shape is encoded in the whorls of our genes. We don't own this body; it grows out of the life that has preceded us.

In his teachings the Buddha gave several reasons why the body cannot be regarded as "mine" or "self," and the simplest one is that we don't have control over the body. In the *Discourse on the Characteristics of Non-self,* the *Anattalankkhana Sutra,* the Buddha explains, "Were it self, the body would not suffer affliction, and one could have of body what one wished, saying 'Let my body be this, let my body be that.'" We can't will our body to change its features, and we can't stop it from being tired, feeling pain, growing sick, aging, or dying. The body has a life of its own.

But the body does not have an independent existence either. For one thing, it is made up of trillions of cells that have their own destiny to work out, and it depends on trillions of bacterial organisms, now doing their own metabolic thing in your mouth, stomach, and intestines. The life of your body also depends heavily on the Earth, at least as a place to lie down on and catch a nap, and also on the heat of the sun to keep you warm and energized. Not least of all, your body's life is nothing without the fuel of oxygen and therefore could not exist without the atmosphere. Your body's most obvious and intimate connection to the world is through one of our primary sources of energy and the very medium through which we move—the air.

AH, BREATH . . .

Mindfulness of body begins with a focus on breathing. Even though it is an essential part of our life-support system, we normally give very little attention to our breath. This is not so strange, considering that breathing doesn't usually demand a lot of attention. It is handled quite efficiently, thank you, by our autonomic nervous system. That is why we can easily get lost in our personal fantasies and forget that none of them would happen without the continual presence of breath. When we make breathing conscious we begin to get in touch with that primary biological fact. At the same time, we can reflect on our connection with the breathing of the biosphere and the great pulses of life moving through us.

In a great many cultures, breath is synonymous with life. The Hindu Upanishads describe a contest between the bodily functions in which the breath wins out and is declared the chief. The Chinese *ch'i* is the universal life force, which is contained and circulated within our own individual breath. In the Old Testament the word for breath, *nephesh,* also means the living spirit. The Greek word *psyche* means "breath-soul," associating breath with a person's essential character.

In almost every school of spiritual liberation a novice will begin with some attention to the process of breathing. As a novice, I had a terrible time keeping attention on my breath. During my early meditation retreats, pop songs used to appear in my head, and I would find my mind singing along with them, no matter how hard I tried to remain focused on my breathing. After a song had started playing in my mind, sometimes I could bring my attention back to my breath for a few minutes, and then suddenly the song would resurface, and it would be a few minutes later in the song. Somewhere beneath the mind that was simply aware of breathing, the band played on.

For forty years I have mostly used breath as the anchor of my meditations. If someone were to count how many hours of my life I have spent focused on breathing they might regard me as somewhat obsessed, fixated on air. I have usually been aware of my breathing at the movement of my abdomen, but at other times I have used a technique that places attention around the nostrils, where one feels the subtle brush of air as it passes in and out across the upper lip and into the nose. Focusing on the nostrils made me especially aware of breath as the meeting place of body and atmosphere.

For a short time in the 1980s I practiced Tibetan Buddhist meditations that follow each breath on its journey into the nose, down through the body, and back out again. This breathing practice is often used in conjunction with the imagination as a way to work with emotions. For instance, in one exercise I practiced visualizing myself inhaling pure white light from the world and exhaling out the dark emotional clouds (anger and greed) from inside me. During another exercise, I imagined inhaling all the negative energies of the world and then purifying them with a compassionate heart and exhaling out the resulting white light of loving-kindness. I was skeptical about these practices at first, but after doing them for a while I found that they connected me to the world through my heart as well as my breath. Our breathing is always a process of give and take, and these exercises just added the affective component.

I breathe in ignorance with wisdom breath but I breathe out
golden mind essence with compassion breath, gently, evenly,
deliberately, peacefully—
Fumigating the universe with mind essence.

JACK KEROUAC, FROM HIS NOTEBOOKS

As we focus on breath, we shift our primary identity away from the mind and psyche, into the substratum of all our life's dramas—life itself. Breath is a less "personal" aspect of our being, and a more fundamental one.

Descartes would have been more accurate if he had said, "I breathe, therefore I am." After all, we can breathe without thinking, but we can't think without breathing. Contemplating the breath, we experience the fact that in a very basic sense we don't live, but rather life lives through us. "Breath happens!"

Although I can alter the rhythm of my breathing somewhat through activity, such as cardiovascular exercise, if I consciously tried to stop breathing I couldn't do it; eventually I would pass out and breathing would resume. Life wants me to live.

While some breathing practices, as in yoga, seek to control the breath or adjust its rhythms, in mindfulness meditation one begins with the simple reflection that (my) breathing happens on its own, and that therefore life is breathing me or breathing through me. That realization can bring about a feeling of intimate connection with the world.

If you sit with your breath for just a few minutes, you can actually feel that with every inhale energy is being pulled in and filling your body, the oxygen flowing to all of your cells and being consumed to keep you alive. Each breath is a gift, a relatively free oxygen lunch offered anew every few seconds.

If you are very attentive you might even sense the intake of what the fifteenth-century Indian poet Kabir called "the breath within the breath," the breath of God, if you so believe, or the great spirit itself, the charge of conscious life emerging from the oxygen fires, the greater mystery in each inhale.

As we experience our breath in meditation, we can also reflect on the fact that we share the air we breathe with everything that lives. In fact, we even share the air with those who lived in the past. Since the oxygen content of our planet is relatively fixed and the oxygen molecules keep recombining and recycling, with your next breath you very well may be inhaling an oxygen molecule that once passed through the body of Abraham, Cleopatra, or the Buddha himself. A molecule in your next breath may well have gone through the body of some club-carrying *Homo habilis,* wandering around a couple of million years ago as bewildered as you and I are today. It turns out we are time-sharing the Earth's oxygen.

With breath reflection we not only connect with other humans, but also with every other form of breathing life: fishes, trees, grasses, birds, mammals, the entire atmosphere. Everything is breathing, trading nutrients and waste in the great gas exchange.

We can also reflect on our breathing as being a daily part of the Earth's breathing. Every single day, all of the life on Earth joins to take one big breath. This happens as plants photosynthesize, creating an increase of oxygen on the daylight side of the planet and a complementary decrease of oxygen on the night side. You might think of planet Earth as an abdomen that revolves rather than contracts, all of Earth's life taking a full breath with each revolution.

Furthermore, every single year the Earth takes a few long deep breaths with the change of seasons, as photosynthesis increases in one of Earth's hemispheres and decreases in the other. Just as the moon moves the tides of the ocean, the sun moves the daily and annual breaths of the Earth.

Some say that even the universe breathes, expanding and contracting with Big Bangs and Big Crunches. Inhale-exhale, light-dark, warm-cold, manifestation-emptiness—it all goes on breathing within you, without you, and through you.

With every inhalation I create the universe, with every exhalation I destroy it.

ZEN SAYING

Aside from revealing our interdependence with the biosphere, awareness of breath also can bring stability and calmness to the mind. In the *Mahasatipatthana Sutra,* the Buddha suggests that meditators experience how "breathing in I calm the entire body . . . breathing out I calm the entire body." Perhaps breathing can be so soothing because it reassures our survival brain—"Yes, life is going on. You can relax."

In Buddhist insight meditation the breath also serves as the place to anchor our attention. In this capacity breath is called the primary object of meditation: we resolve to be aware of breath, and only of breath. When we intend to be focused only on breathing, we can then notice when other experiences pull us away. We begin to see how the mind runs off on its own, and the places to which it runs. After many meditation sessions of being quite frustrated by my inability to stay focused on my breathing, I realized that the difficulty was actually a gift, revealing to me how my mind works.

By attending to the breath, we also begin to train our mind for further exploration. The breath becomes a whetstone on which to sharpen mental concentration, teaching us how to focus mindfulness on arising and passing phenomena without reaction or personal identification. After using the breath—a relatively neutral object—as training wheels, we can apply the mind's new skills to more personally sensitive aspects of our being.

EXERCISES

❧ Breathing Lessons ❧

Breathing in, I am still water. Noticing the temporary nature of governments, I breathe out.

THICH NHAT HANH

You can practice a few minutes of breath meditation at any time throughout the day, as often as you want. One of the advantages of breath meditation is that it can be done anywhere and in any posture. Paying attention to just two or three breaths—with simple reflection on them as the greater pulse of life— can bring you a relaxed feeling of simple presence and aliveness.

The Basic Meditation on Breathing (*Anapanasati*)

To begin this practice, be seated in a comfortable position, and after making a commitment to meditate for a certain period of time (ten minutes as a minimum) bring your awareness to the *experience* of breathing. Settle awareness on the movements in the region of your abdomen as air gets drawn into your body and then released. Without any intentional comment or analysis, become fully present with each breath. As much as possible, let the breathing be natural.

At some point, instead of watching the breath, let your consciousness sink into the actual sensations in your abdominal region. You might sense the abdomen as a hammock, with consciousness riding on the rhythm of its movements.

To experience more clearly that your breath is happening on its own, at the end of each exhale release any anticipation of the next breath. Let yourself be surprised by each breath as it begins. In this way you come to realize that the universe is breathing you. Or that the universe is breathing *through* you.

Remember to practice mindfulness—a nonreactive, non-interfering awareness. Just make a sincere intention to stay present with your breathing. If you then notice that your mind has wandered, simply bring your attention back to the breath with as little comment and analysis as possible. If you notice some self-judgment about getting lost in thought, look at it this way: if you were sincere about wanting to be aware only of your breath, then it wasn't *you* that decided to get lost in thought or distracted. The mind wandered off on its own. It is quite natural for human minds to wander and think, so there is no cause for blame.

If you do hear your mind being self-critical, then just notice that. No need to be critical of being self-critical. That is the beginning of the infinite regression of self-criticism.

After making a sincere intention to be aware of each breath, just notice what else occurs. Remember, one way that you are using the breath is as a platform from which to explore the far reaches of your mind and psyche. As you get pushed and pulled, here and there, you are learning how instincts and habits are functioning in your life.

Whenever your mind settles down a little, you could begin to explore your breathing more closely. Focus on the very subtlest beginnings of each breath, and the final wisps of the exhale. Be aware of the space between breaths, noticing what your mind does during those empty moments. See if you can stay attentive to each microsecond of your breathing. In this way you begin to sharpen your mental concentration.

Co-Breathing

At some point in a meditation session, open your eyes and look around you at a green plant in your house or at the trees and grasses outside. Reflect on the fact that with every breath we feed the plants and get fed by them. Doing this reflection even a few times can infuse you with a new feeling of intimacy with the plant world. You aren't just being fed by them, you are also feeding them. As you walk outside you may sense yourself a little more connected to the tree in your yard, even if you don't go to hug it. You may feel your role in the breathing of the biosphere, your part in the pulse of all life.

The breath is used in many other ways in meditation practices, most notably for working with strong emotions. This method, which involves the use of visualization or imagination, will be described later on in the book.

> "Breathing in, I liberate my mind. Breathing out, I liberate my mind." The meditator practices like this. "Breathing in, I observe the impermanence of all phenomena. Breathing out, I observe the impermanence of all phenomena. "The meditator practices like this."
>
> THE BUDDHA, ANAPANASATI SUTRA

Heartbeat

Although this practice is not included in the traditional meditations on the body, bringing conscious awareness to your heartbeat for a few minutes can provide some of the same benefits as awareness of breath. If you are very still and attentive you might be able to feel the pulse of heartbeat throughout the body. If not, take hold of your wrist or place your hand on your heart. Just feel the vital pulsations for a while.

Reflect on the fact that all living things have a pulse. Have you ever seen a film or video of one-celled organisms as they twitch with life? It's the spasms of the protoplasm. And as you feel your heart pulse, do you experience any rhythmic kinship with those cells? That twitching, set down in the very early days, is nothing less than the back beat over which all of life is played. Even if you can't keep a beat, you are keeping the beat.

REINCARNATED

Reflections on the Body

After the breath meditations, the *Mahasatipatthana Sutra* continues with a series of exercises that can offer us experiential knowledge of the physical body. Here again, we are invited to explore various aspects of our evolutionary inheritance—the constant metabolism taking place inside of us, our skeletal and muscular structure, the sensations and movements of the body. These are not exercises to stretch or strengthen the body, but to examine its deepest nature.

One exercise has us focus on "both arising and vanishing phenomena in the body." If you bring concentrated attention to any part of your body, you will eventually feel tingling, twitching, flowing, or bubbling sensations, evidence of the natural processes taking place inside of you at every moment, usually beneath your awareness. You may be experiencing digestion, or metabolic activity, or the tingling of nerves as messages are whisked around through your body. When we consciously experience these sensations we become familiar with our body as a process rather than a thing and recognize that its life goes on within us and mostly without us.

Another instruction tells us simply to have mindfulness that "there is body," and then to practice awareness of this body at rest and in motion. The instructions say that a meditator "when walking, knows that he [or she] is walking, when standing knows that he is standing. . . . In whatever way the body is disposed, he knows that that is how it is." And when the meditator begins to move, "when going forward or back he is clearly aware of what he is doing. In bending and stretching . . . in eating, drinking, chewing, and savoring, in passing excrement or urine . . . in walking, standing, sitting, falling asleep, and waking up, in speaking or in staying silent, he is clearly aware of what he is doing."

These are existential practices. They are telling us to be aware and fully present with each of our activities. Ordinarily we let the body walk, stand, urinate, and chew *for us,* without our conscious attention, so that we can continue doing what we consider to be more important, which is usually thinking about something else. By meditating on our physical posture and movement, we become aware of how much our mind is split off from our body. With these exercises those who live only inside their head can practice incarnating again.

With these exercises we also begin to realize that the body is full of unease, in a nearly constant state of restlessness, and that often the unease is subconsciously motivating our behavior. We see that often the tail is indeed wagging the dog.

As we explore the body with mindfulness, I believe that we touch some deep intelligence that informs us of the evolutionary nature of our physical existence. We begin to sense the long lineage of life forms that have shaped our limbs and our senses. As we will discover later when we do a guided reflection on the skeleton, the deeper we go within the body, the more connections we will find with all of life.

You Slime Bag!

Another reflection on the body from the *Mahasatipatthana Sutra* has us examine thirty-two different body parts, piece by piece. Traditionally this exercise is used as an antidote for people who get lost in appearances, those with a lot of sexual drive, or those who are vain about their body. The sutra calls it a reflection on "the repulsive," although an equally valid translation is "the not-beautiful."

Basically, this meditation reveals that what we consider beautiful in one form might seem disgusting in another. An example one of my teachers used to offer was that someone's hair might seem attractive to you, unless a few of those hairs got into your soup. When viewed separately, the different parts of the body will generally appear to us as either neutral or to some degree unappealing.

The reflection leads us into our own soup, as the meditator is instructed to review the body "from the soles of the feet upward and from the scalp downward, enclosed by the skin and full of manifold impurities." We are told to name and reflect upon "head-hairs, body-hairs, nails, teeth, skin, flesh, sinews, bones, bone-marrow, kidneys, heart, liver . . . bile, phlegm, pus, blood, sweat, fat, tears." We are asked to look unsparingly at what constitutes our body.

In the course of their spiritual journey, many Western Buddhists that I know have skipped over this meditation exercise. Those I ask about it say they view it as a denigration of life. Having bypassed it myself for many years, I began meditating on the parts of the body after being taught the practice by a quick-witted Thai forest monk named Ajahn Jumnien, who came to teach at Spirit Rock Meditation Center in 1996.

Ajahn Jumnien first had us move our mindfulness through the skeleton, muscles, and sinews. I found this process rather delightful, just feeling the architectural wonders of my body. But eventually Jumnien began to guide us into a contemplation of our bowels, and as he did so my mood shifted a little. I began to feel a hint of revulsion.

The body may be the temple of my soul, but do I really have to look at the plumbing?

Jumnien told us to *feel* the bag of our guts, tightly encased by skin, and full of liquids and slippery organs. Then he had us use our imagination to dissect and examine the different organs. "Look at what's inside there," he said, "the small intestines wrapped in something that looks like sausage-skin holding a slimy mass of half-digested food, the stuff you see when you throw up. And there's the reddish-gray liver, full of toxins and dangerous waste, and the bladder storing urine, and the large intestines holding your feces."

We don't want to acknowledge that all of this slimy stuff is inside of us, substances that would make us sick if we could see them. So, we avoid the reality of our digestive system as much as possible, just as we avoid the shadows of our psyche. Luckily, we have skin covering our guts, but, just in case, we also dress ourselves up colorfully and beautifully. Perhaps we paint the skin of our faces, in part to distract attention from our underbelly. I noticed, however, that Ajahn Jumnien guided us through our innards without any disgust or aversion in his voice. Even though one of the purposes of this meditation is to loosen our attachment to our bodies, it is not intended to create any distaste or physical self-loathing. The meditation is simply designed to break through the idealized story about who we are. It is not a disparaging look at ourselves, merely a realistic one.

As I continued the contemplation, my own revulsion began to dissipate. Through the lens of mindfulness—nonjudgmental awareness—I was able to accept and honor these nitty-gritty conditions of life.

> *Be humble for you are made of dung. Be noble for you are made of stars.*
>
> SERBIAN SAYING

WHO AM I?
ELEMENTARY, MY DEAR WATSON
A Reflection on the Elements

Shall I not have intelligence with the earth? Am I not partly leaves and vegetable mould myself?

HENRY DAVID THOREAU

The classical Buddhist meditations on the elements of earth, air, fire, and water allow us to experience directly our physical kinship with all of nature. In fact, our bodies are composed of the same material elements as the earth—carbon, nitrogen, oxygen, sulfur, and minerals. Our bones are made of calcium phosphate, the clay of earth molded into this human shape. Our blood is also the Earth's blood, the salty waters of the ocean infused with fire and splashed up on shore.

Many cultures throughout history have recognized earth, air, fire, and water as the basic elements of nature, and many have worshipped one or more of them in their religions. Important in Buddhist practice is the fact that each of the four elements has a quality and function that can be experienced inside us. Earth has the feeling of hardness and solidity, and its function is to support. Water can be felt in its aspect of cohesion and flowing, and its function is to bind. Fire or the lack of it brings changes in temperature, and its function is to ripen or mature. Air can be felt as expansion or contraction and has the function of motion.

Like awareness of breath, the Buddhist reflections on earth, air, fire, and water can help shift our identity from the personal to the universal: we learn that we are quite literally one with the oceans, the atmosphere, the sun, and the Earth.

Earth Born

> *Life does not exist on Earth's surface, so much as it is Earth's surface.*
>
> LYNN MARGULIS AND DORIAN FAGAN, *WHAT IS LIFE?*

The reflections begin with the earth element, which is characterized by solidity, hardness, mass. You can experience these qualities at this very moment in the shape and weight of your body. You can feel your body as a relatively compact mass of matter, just like the earth.

The earth element within us becomes clear when we begin to examine our body in relation to the planet itself. While we often reflect on the moon's sway over us—our psyche and blood affected by its changing phases—we seldom are conscious of the more direct and powerful influence of the Earth, probably because it is so constant and so near. Its name is gravity.

Just now, whatever position you are in, become aware of the Earth beneath you (or beneath your chair or the floor). After a few minutes of feeling as if you are *on* the Earth, reflect that instead the mysterious force of gravity is actually holding you here. You might feel it as a gentle tugging, a pull, or even a fond embrace. You are always being held to the Earth by this force when sitting, lying, walking. You couldn't let go even if you cared to. As simple as this reflection may seem, it can shift our sense of where, and who, we are. The experience of gravity might even pull down the pants of your pride a little. Yes, you can move around on your own, but due to gravity you can't move very far, and you can't move very fast.

The real shift of awareness comes, however, when you begin to sense the fact—substantiated by chemistry and evolutionary sciences— that you are not so much *on* the Earth as you are *of* the Earth. If you believe in the theory of evolution, then you must acknowledge that you literally emerged from the Earth and its seas, the source to which all life has been traced. If you agree that life on this planet begins with the sun's energy igniting the essential chemical compounds bathing in sea water, then the Earth is indeed your birth mother, and her seas were your amniotic fluids. If you can't accept that, then you must believe that humans were dropped down here from outer space or somehow formed independently from the rest of life. Neither story seems any less miraculous than the other.

Take just a few minutes and see if you can experience your body as part of the Earth. Begin by once again feeling your body supported by the Earth. Feel yourself tightly connected to it like a magnet.

Now shift your perspective to imagine that your body is a living extension of the Earth, having grown out of it. Feel that you are an earth sprout that has gained a lot of mobility. You emerged from the Earth like a child but have broken somewhat free of your mother. You will always remain connected, however, and in the end your body will inevitably return home.

Here Comes the Sun

> Life is a solar phenomenon. . . . The entire unfolding of evolution is a response to an exportable excess, a growing surplus of sun-derived energy.
> LYNN MARGULIS AND DORIAN FAGAN, *WHAT IS LIFE?*

Life is warm. Death is cold. The fire element inside you makes all the difference.

One of the two most basic formulas of biology is called the equation of photosynthesis, which describes how plants make foods out of sunlight, carbon dioxide, and water. The other vital formula is the equation of burning, which explains how plants and animals transform that captured sunlight into the heat energy that fuels their lives. Everything alive is burning. That is a fundamental law of nature.

To experience the fire element, become aware of the heat of your body. You can easily feel that heat inside, as well as its radiation around the surface of your skin. As you feel the fire in and around you, perhaps you can also sense it energizing your life—and simultaneously consuming it. As the Buddhist texts say, the fire element matures and ripens us.

Reflect on the fact that much of our body heat comes from simply standing next to the fire of the sun, our great space-heater. The sun's fire warms our skin as well as the air we breathe. Most of the heat we feel inside, however, enters us through the food we eat, grown under that powerful light. The more we can experience our heat and energy as the sun's fire, the more intimately we feel connected to the universe, or at the very least to our own solar system. Our warm bloodedness is made out of sunbeams.

Water Me!

> Life is the story of bodies that learned to contain the sea.
>
> WILLIAM BRYANT LOGAN,
> DIRT: THE ECSTATIC SKIN OF THE EARTH

One of the essential ingredients for life as we know it is water. Approximately 75 percent of your body's mass is made up of water, or at least reduces down to it.

When you taste your own blood or sweat you are tasting the ocean. Life began in the sea, and its water is chemically similar to the liquid flowing through your veins and flesh. You contain the waves of the ocean that splashed up on shore and eventually walked away.

In the Buddhist literature the water element is characterized by cohesion and fluidity. As such, it provides the medium of transportation—packing and shipping—for many of the chemical and mineral nutrients that are necessary to your body's life.

You can feel the fluidity of the water element through the flow of your blood, as it gets pumped around through its channels in the body by your heart. You can also experience the water element inside you by tasting the moisture in your mouth or feeling the slipperiness in your eyes or the mucous membranes of your nose. You can feel it by simply patting your belly, or by noticing the watery nature of the flesh in the muscles of your arms or legs.

This watery nature—our real liquidity—is a sign of our vitality. As we get older the percentage of water in the body steadily decreases. If you live long enough you will quite literally dry up. If you are then cremated and have your ashes scattered, you may also blow away.

Airborne

The air element is characterized by movement and can be felt prominently and vitally inside your body, especially in your breathing. With every breath, the air brings the essential oxygen molecules into your body and hauls carbon dioxide molecules back out to fertilize the plants. In any breath you can reflect on this vital exchange and feel your connection to the greater cycles of the planet.

You can also experience the air element all around you. We normally don't notice air, just as the fish doesn't notice the water, but if you pay close attention you can sense it, or even feel its touch directly on your hands or face or on the surface of any exposed skin.

You can also feel the air by moving your arm or hand through it, or by walking through it. Next time you move around or take a walk, become aware of the air as the medium through which you are moving. As you walk be aware of the air parting or flowing around you. Over the next few weeks or months—as an exercise in awareness of the basics of your life—occasionally try to give more regard to the *feel* of this medium in which you live.

The air element can also be experienced within us as a feeling of either expansion or contraction. Expansion can be felt as a spaciousness or lightness, while contraction is a heavy, closed, or enfolded feeling.

Mental life—the buzzing sensation that comes from the brain—can sometimes be felt as a quality of the air element. Tibetan Buddhists often speak of thoughts and moods as winds, messages riding on the air currents, appearing out of the wilderness of our karma. Sometimes they are thunderstorms that sweep in over our lives for months at a time. Other times they are cool breezes of peace that soothe the inner brow.

These reflections on the elements are usually done in silent meditation, with an emphasis on feeling the qualities of the element under consideration. Although they are typically practiced only on occasion, people who work with these exercises report feeling more embedded in nature and experiencing shifts of identity. These exercises are basic primers of evolutionary wisdom, giving us an experience of ourselves as earthy—as Earthlings.

THE ETERNAL SCULPTOR

In school we learn of ice ages in one set of books and of "history" in another and fail to see how the two are connected; we fail to perceive, therefore, that beneath the surface tremors of our lives there are much deeper and more powerful forces at work that in the end affect us and all our fellow creatures at least as profoundly as the events of day-to-day.

COLIN TUDGE, *THE TIME BEFORE HISTORY*

Our physical being is not only composed of the elements of earth, air, fire, and water, but has also been shaped by them, as has every activity of our lives. Our bodies and brains, the way we walk and talk, the way we build our houses and roads and obtain our food have all been carved or coaxed from the life force by elemental demands: by the colliding of tectonic plates and the upheavals of mountains, by great masses of water flooding the Earth or crushing it in ice. Changes in the elements have motivated life to move from fins to fingers and from jungle to plains. Fluctuating Earth temperatures and climates—the fire and air elements—have made us shiver, sweat, and move across the planet looking for shelter or shade, and new sources of nourishment. Recent scientific discoveries reveal how life "co-evolves" with the elements, a modern concept similar to an ancient Buddhist idea of the interdependent appearance of all phenomena.

> *Mountains' walking is just like human walking. Accordingly, do not doubt mountains' walking even though it does not look the same as human walking. You should penetrate these words. If you doubt mountains' walking, you do not know your own walking.*
>
> ZEN MASTER DOGEN,
> *THE MOUNTAINS AND WATERS SUTRA*

In the eighteenth century, many people thought the scientists were crazy when they began speculating that over time whole continents of land had moved great distances over the Earth's surface. We now have evidence from carbon dating and other geologic research techniques that, in fact, where you are right now was at one time somewhere else on the planet. If you had stayed alive in one place long enough you might have been able to see the world without ever leaving home.

With every major movement of land mass or shift of climate, life is dramatically reshaped. Big changes in elemental forces send shock waves through the worldwide flora and fauna. As we consider our own body, we might reflect on the fact that the most critical steps in its creation can be correlated with major environmental change. Scientists believe that an abundance of algae-produced oxygen along with great upheavals of land masses nearly six hundred million years ago triggered the Cambrian explosion—also known as biology's Big Bang or the Big

Birth—which marks the first appearance of many forms of life, including multicellular animals with skeleton-like structures.

Geologic events have molded us. A meteor crashing to earth sixty-five million years ago has been linked to atmospheric changes that caused the extinction of the dinosaurs, allowing for the subsequent evolution of larger mammals, present company included.

More recent geologic and atmospheric events are associated with the specific emergence of our species, *Homo sapiens*. The landmass of Africa, for instance, was dramatically altered by tectonic forces twelve to fifteen million years ago, creating highlands in Kenya and Ethiopia some nine thousand feet in altitude and producing the Great Rift Valley. Some evolutionary scientists believe that the Great Rift Valley erected an east-west barrier to the existing animal populations. As a result, populations of the common ancestors of humans and apes were divided, and each group began evolving under different conditions. According to French anthropologist Yves Coppens, "The western descendants of these common ancestors pursued their adaptation to life in a humid, arboreal milieu; these are the apes. The eastern descendants of these same common ancestors, in contrast, invented a completely new repertoire in order to adapt to their new life in an open environment; these are the humans." A major force of evolution has also been temperature—the fire element—and especially the lack of it. At least ten times in the past million years, the Earth has cooled off enough to create what we call an ice age. Ice glaciers the width of continents and as deep as mountain ranges have covered North America and Eurasia. The ice solidified so much water that sea levels fell worldwide, completely draining the Mediterranean Sea several times and creating land bridges that linked such places as Alaska and Siberia, Indonesia and mainland Asia. The resulting migration of plant and animal species into new environments was further stimulus for evolutionary change.

The ice ages are now recognized as a major force in the emergence of *Homo sapiens*. Scientists now believe that our particular biological family, Hominidae, came into existence during the colder weather of the late Miocene, seven million years ago, and that our genus, *Homo,* along with those of cattle and gazelles, came into existence during another cooling period two-and-a-half million years ago. Our tremendous human energy and ingenuity seem to have something to do with the fact that we suddenly grew cold. Perhaps consciousness and the opposable thumb were originally designed as tools for shoveling snow.

> *We, mankind, arose amidst the wandering of the ice and marched with it. We are in some sense shaped by it, as it has shaped the stones. Perhaps our very fondness for the building of stone alignments, dolmens, and pyramids reveals unconsciously an ancient heritage from the ice itself, the earth shaper.*
>
> COLIN TUDGE, *THE TIME BEFORE HISTORY*

DANCES WITH ELEMENTS
Reflections

Exercises in the Tibetan Buddhist tradition advise students to sit near a river or gaze into the sky, and to focus on the "flowing" quality of natural phenomena, reflecting that we humans are also of that nature. Near a river or ocean we can witness constant movement, as well as the slow but sure transformation of earth by water. Near hills or mountains we can regard the latest posture in the "walking" of the land, and how that affects all the other elements. The land's shape is always influencing the weather patterns and flow of water, which in turn determine where the plants will grow thickest and where humans and other animals will build their houses. "And the green grass grew all 'round, all 'round. . . ."

Notice how everything is in motion. The light is always changing, letting us know that the planet is always moving in relation to the sun. We can experience shifts of wind, humidity, and temperature, and notice the daily or weekly changes in the plant life around us. The landscape and climate give us a continual lesson in impermanence.

Reflect on the probability that wherever you are at this very moment was at one time underwater and may have been part of a mountain range or once covered by ice. Wherever you are was once located in a different latitude and longitude of Earth as well. What is now North America, for instance, was once Laurentia, a huge island located near the equator and surrounded by a vast ocean, with most of its land mass submerged. Some two hundred million years later, almost all of the land masses of earth were joined together in one vast continent known as Pangaea, or "all earth." That arrangement did not last long, and we can be thankful that it didn't because of the lack of good beaches.

∞

Consider the critical importance of our distance from the sun on who we are today. If the Earth had been a little smaller or larger, or for some other reason had settled into an orbit either closer to or farther from the sun, we may have evolved as entirely different life forms, or not evolved at all. A little closer and the Earth would have been so hot that we might have been underground, wormlike creatures; a little farther and we might look something like woolly mammoths, and all be living in tiny colonies near the equator.

Consider the house you live in, the clothing you wear, the food you eat, your occupation and diversions, and how they are conditioned by the climate in which you live. Differences in air temperature, soil conditions, and availability of water determine how we build our shelters, how we cultivate our food, and even the songs we sing and the gods that we worship.

Other species of life have also helped shape us, since we evolved in part to cope with them and find our place in a world that included them, but all living things were fashioned by geologic and atmospheric forces. Earth, air, fire, and water play major roles in our collective autobiography, and when we don't notice or feel that connection we are diminished in both wisdom and wonder. We lose sight of our origins, and our place in the scheme of things.

> *Oh, what a catastrophe, what maiming of love when it was made a personal, merely personal feeling, taken away from the rising and the setting of the sun, and cut off from the magic connection of the solstice and equinox! This is what is the matter with us, we are bleeding at the roots, because we are cut off from the earth and sun and stars, and love is a grinning mockery, because, poor blossom, we plucked it from its stem on the tree of Life, and expected it to keep on blooming in our civilized vase on the table.*
>
> D.H. LAWRENCE, *PHOENIX II*

THE KARMA OF EVOLUTION

> *The Buddha pronounced this round of Causes and Effects, this universal chain where never was a beginning, to be the Law.*
>
> VISUDDHIMAGGA

The Buddha directed us to examine our relationship to the elements as one way of recognizing that our body has no separate, independent existence. He is encouraging us to become scientists of the self and to do research into all of the processes involved in creating our body, feelings, perceptions, and consciousness. His instructions were based in part on one of his own era's causal principles known as the law of karma.

In Sanskrit, the word *karma* means "to do" or "to make," and refers to the fact that every action is followed by consequences. In common usage, karma has become synonymous with destiny and is often referred to as a person's inherited circumstances and temperament. "You've got to work through your own karma," as the saying goes. Karma can even be understood as the journey of the soul as it emerges from a mysterious past or realm to become embodied and seek resolution or fulfillment in this particular world.

The Hindu law of karma, which was current when the Buddha lived, was concerned primarily with an individual's expressed actions in the world, and how the consequences of those actions would affect that person's destiny, even into future lives. For example, if one person hurt another, he or she set up a chain of events that would inevitably end in the first person experiencing pain. The idea is summed up in today's slang as "everything that goes around, comes around."

The Buddha added a whole new dimension to this causal law by emphasizing that karma is also a psychological conditioning process that operates in this very life. He recognized that our thoughts as well as our actions have consequences, and that those consequences also take place in our own mind. Whenever we think or act out of greed or hatred, regardless of the results in the world around us, we strengthen those particular instincts or habits within ourselves. Since greed and hatred are sources of our suffering, we don't want to reinforce those habits. Conversely, by cultivating positive states of mind, such as equanimity or compassion, we create seeds of happiness for ourselves. With every movement of mind, we are conditioning our future states of consciousness.

As a scientist of the self, the Buddha gave a very precise description of how this law of karma works in our lives. His understanding is summarized in the Sanskrit phrase *pratitya samutpada,* which translates as "dependent co-arising," and is outlined as twelve interlinking processes that condition our reality. Simply put, because we have a body, senses, and consciousness, we will have the experience of contact with the world. As a result of that contact some kind of sensation will be produced in our bodies (we are sentient beings). When sensations arise, we feel them as either pleasant, unpleasant, or neutral. These feelings normally lead to reactions of craving or aversion—we want more or we want less—and our reactions then turn into full-blown emotions of greed or hatred, which we feel inside as discontent or suffering. This entire sequence usually takes place beneath conscious awareness, and we don't seem to recognize this mental process itself as the source of our misery. It is therefore our ignorance—often named in Buddhist texts as the first of the twelve links—that is the root cause that keeps us turning on the wheel of suffering. This simple schema of dependent co-arising is a profound acknowledgment of our human condition.

Meanwhile, some schools of Buddhism place more emphasis on universal causality, and the notion that all elements and phenomena are mutually interacting and influencing each other throughout the cosmos through all of time. This universal view, in contrast to the twelve-link wheel of karma, can be compared to the way modern physicists understand the scientific laws of causality. On the surface level, the physicist recognizes that the universe is explainable in mechanistic terms, with one billiard ball hitting another and causing the second one to move, but on the subatomic level (through quantum processes) everything is also conditioning everything else all at once.

The Buddha advised us not to try to separate out all the specifics in the tangle of our karma, saying that it was an "imponderable." We could never isolate or measure all of the events and processes that have produced this particular here and now. It is very important, however, to see the principle of karma, the fact that nothing arises independently of causes and conditions. We then begin to recognize ourselves and each moment of our experience as interwoven with all creation.

Although we may never be able to unravel the entire magic carpet of the causal field, the modern story of evolution may at least be exposing a few of the threads. Through this story we can see clearly that our lives are the temporary creation of great forces moving through time.

The scientific story of evolution can even offer a new angle on the idea of reincarnation. Life itself seems to reincarnate in form after form, with new methods of locomotion, perception, or types of consciousness. The human condition can be seen as our shared incarnation, part of our common "evolutionary karma."

Evolutionary science is even showing us some of the faces of our previous collective incarnations. You can see, twitching away on a petri dish, a living example of past life as a single-celled organism. In a water-breathing fish you can imagine a version of yourself in a previous life, swimming through the single ocean that once covered the Earth. You can perhaps recognize yourself more easily as a great ape, with lumbering walk and questioning stare, or even more easily in the paleontologists' pictures of the skull and bones of a particular *Homo habilis,* one of your past lives when, by definition, you were a handy person.

Our shared past lives can be even more easily recognized by looking at individual development in the womb. Within nine months we develop from a single cell to a complex mammal, keeping the adaptations we might still need, discarding those that are unnecessary, such as gills, and downsizing others, such as the acute olfactory region of the brain, since smell is no longer so essential to our survival as humans.

In the book *What Is Life?,* authors Dorion Sagan and Lynn Margulis suggest the depth of our inheritance: "We share more than 98 percent of our genes with chimpanzees, sweat fluids reminiscent of seawater, and crave sugar that provided our ancestors with energy three billion years before the first space station had evolved. We carry our past with us."

The idea that we have previous lives in the evolutionary past can even extend beyond biology, into the realm of elemental forces and cycles. After all, the entire Earth was once a cloud of gas, and later a cooling, molten rock. Were we not part of those as well? As Thich Nhat

Hanh writes in *The Heart of Understanding,* "As I look more deeply, I can see that in a former life I was a cloud. And I was a rock. This is not poetry; it is science. This is not a question of belief in reincarnation. This is the history of life on earth."

Although there is no indication that people knew of evolution in the Buddha's time, there are many legendary stories of the Buddha himself appearing in the form of different species in the lifetimes before he became the Buddha. These Jataka folk tales depict the Buddha-to-be as, among other creatures, a tree, a snake, a deer, and an elephant. The good deeds and wisdom he displayed in each of these former lifetimes can be seen as a prelude—perhaps even a precondition—to a birth in which he could achieve full awakening of consciousness. The concept of life evolving is not foreign to Buddhism, whether it be told in legends of reincarnation, or as the interconnection of all things in the universe, or through the core belief in the possibility of transformation in this life.

> *Not yet having become a Buddha, this ancient pine tree dreaming.*
>
> ISSA

Life's Biography: The Early Years

If you focus your attention at this moment on any part of your body, you will eventually feel a great flux and flow of minuscule sensations. What you are feeling are the processes of life happening inside your body. This life may not just be your own, however. Taking into consideration the discoveries of microbiology, you just might be feeling the activity of trillions of other individuals—single-celled organisms—who are living, migrating, metabolizing, and dying within your body's passageways at this very moment.

With this kind of specific information, modern science offers us a new way to reflect on our body's evolution. The meditators of the

Buddha's time could feel evidence of natural processes taking place inside them, but they probably had no idea that the sensations may have included the movement of other forms of life. When we ask the question "Who am I?" science can point us toward our specific connections not only with the elements but with elementary *life*. A brief review of life's early history will guide and support our spiritual practice of self-awareness and liberation.

> *We have seen the totality of living things as a continuous slowly advancing sheet of protoplasm out of which nature has been ceaselessly trying to carve systems complete and harmonious in themselves, isolable from all other things, and independent. But she has never been completely successful: the systems are never quite cut off, for each must take its origin in one or more pieces of a previous system. In a sense, therefore, the whole organic world constitutes a single great individual.*

> JULIAN HUXLEY,
> *The Individual in the Animal Kingdom*

As close as scientists can figure, this mysterious quality of things we call "life" was born three-and-a-half billion years ago in the oceans. Seawater contained all the basic ingredients and when heated by the sun became a living soup-stock.

Life stayed in the ocean for a couple of billion years until some vital force or evolutionary demand forced it up onto the land. In stages, of course. But this process of moving from sea to land was probably the biggest single adjustment life has ever had to make. The equivalent would be for humans to now return to the ocean to live or take up permanent residence in outer space. The medium is the message.

Humans are descended from a large classification of beings called "animals," and while it is relatively easy to poke fun at the idea of "getting in touch with your animal nature," there is nonetheless a profound wisdom to be gained by acknowledging this aspect of our identity. The Buddha taught people to pay attention to the most basic elements of their existence, and we can now see clearly through the evolutionary sciences that our human condition is also an animal condition; our lives carry the demands and constraints of all animals.

One reason we are classified as animals is the fact that we must eat other living beings. No judgment intended: it's only natural. An animal is an organism that does not photosynthesize and therefore must eat other organisms in order to get the energy to live. As animals, we have to eat either organisms that photosynthesize or organisms that eat other organisms that photosynthesize. Getting the sun's power inside our bodies is essential to animal life.

Eating other organisms means that we have to go out into the world and hunt them down or dig them out of the ground or pick them off trees. That's one reason why our life is so hard. An animal has to be *animated* and move around a lot just to accomplish what plants can manage by staying in one place and photosynthesizing. In comparison to plants, the animals' system doesn't seem very efficient—until recently, when humans could get into their cars and drive to the supermarket. That is animal efficiency for you.

Another characteristic of animals that holds tremendous influence over our behavior is the fact that it takes cells from two of us to reproduce. The female's egg gets fertilized by a male of the species, which turns the egg into a growing ball of cells, an embryo. One-celled organisms can reproduce on their own by dividing and don't need to develop charming personalities in order to woo other cells (unless we are overlooking some interesting activity on those microscope slides).

But we are not so different from those cells, really. They too have their functional boundaries, ways to communicate with the outside world, and ways to maintain and propagate their existence. Their basic message and raison d'être, which we now carry deep inside of us, is to go forth and multiply. That may have been useful for cells, because innumerable trillions of them could easily be supported by the Earth. But as satirist Darryl Henriques points out, "When it comes to humans, God should have instructed us just to go forth and add."

Sea Shells, Me Cells

> *The blueprints, detailed instructions, and job orders*
> *for building you from scratch would fill about 1,000*
> *encyclopedia volumes if written out in English. Yet every cell*
> *in your body has a set of these encyclopedias.*
>
> CARL SAGAN, *THE DEMON-HAUNTED WORLD*

Scientists agree that the first form of physical life was a single cell, which first appeared roughly 3.8 billion years ago. Single-celled organisms lived alone on the planet for more than 2 billion years before any other life form emerged from the soup, and these types of single-celled beings are still alive today. In that sense they can be understood as the most successful of all life forms, and an argument could be made that all subsequent life evolved just to serve them. To many of the one-celled organisms, we are nothing more than moving feedlots.

Only in recent decades have scientists discovered the enormous evolutionary contribution of early cell life, and how it created the vital groundwork for many aspects of both our bodies and behavior. Microbiologists are now showing us just how correct the Buddha was when he said, "This body does not belong to you. . . . It is the result of previous activity."

During their first two billion years of active life on Earth, for instance, single-celled organisms developed all the essential chemical systems that sustain us today—photosynthesis, fermentation, oxygen breathing, and the fixing of atmospheric nitrogen into proteins. Without these developments, our planet would be as lifeless as the moon, with no air and no soil. The single-celled organisms prepared our world for us and prepared us for our world.

Lynn Margulis, distinguished professor of biology at the University of Massachusetts, has written: "Far from leaving microorganisms behind on an evolutionary ladder, we are both surrounded by them and composed of them." She points out that we carry around inside of us trillions upon trillions of single-celled beings. Indeed, the number of bacteria inside your mouth at this moment is greater than the number of people who have ever lived. The implications that Margulis draws from this kind of scientific information echoes the Buddha's understanding, as in her observation, "Our concept of the individual is totally warped. All of us are walking communities."

Not only do the microorganisms inhabit us, but they also form the very foundation of our physical existence. The biologists have discovered that bacteria have the unique ability to join themselves together to create new lifeforms, in a process known as symbiogenesis. The importance of symbiogenesis in evolution has only recently been discovered, in large part due to Margulis's work. She claims that it was symbiogenesis that created the microscopic beings called protists, one of the first and most important forms of complex life.

The tiny, multicelled protists are considered responsible for inventing locomotion, our form of digestion, visual and other sensory systems, chromosomal DNA, the ability to create bones, and the first gendered system of reproduction. We should build a statue—perhaps in UN Plaza—of a protist or two, in spite of the fact that they are generally considered quite ugly. Their struggles for survival have made us who we are today.

None of these early creatures was anything more than a bundle of biochemicals wrapped up in a membrane bag. Even so, in their makeup and activity, we can recognize the inception of a new quality in the universe. These ancient gelatinous specks of matter showed the beginnings of self-interest and purpose. They had established barriers, definite, sustainable boundaries, between themselves and the outside world. And although the heady heights of human intellect and introspection lay almost four billion years away, even the most elementary of lifeforms harbored information about what was part of their own constitution and what was not. Thus, the foundations for dualism—the belief in the separation of self and the rest of the world—were laid.

DAVID DARLING, *ZEN PHYSICS*

The Buddha could have pointed to the early evolution of cellular life as an excellent example of dependent co-arising, revealing that every aspect of our experience arises out of an uncountable number of past causes and conditions. According to Lynn Margulis, even our vaunted ability to think has some of its roots in the history of cell life.

To understand this connection, we first take Margulis's theory of symbiogenesis as it addresses the ability of life to move around. The theory says that cells first became mobile by merging with whiplashing spirochetes, which are simple bacteria. The bodies of spirochetes pulse in a wave-like motion, and at some point in the early history of life they apparently began to attach themselves to larger cells with nuclei. This helped the larger cells to get around, and the spirochetes in turn got to live with a bigger mouth and stomach. It was a mutually beneficial exchange—motion for mass.

We contain the DNA of those spirochetes, and Margulis claims that in many ways our lives are built around their legacy. For instance, she looked at human spermatozoa with their whip-like tails, and then at the long axon and dendrite tentacles extending from our brain and nerve cells, and recognized the close similarities between these structures and the spirochetes. Margulis now believes that all cell tails are produced by spirochete DNA. In other words, our ability to procreate and communicate is based on the shape of one-celled beings. The movement of messages through our brain—our thoughts—can be understood as a refinement of a basic microbial design.

If this theory proves to be true—and there is increasing evidence to support it—we have found another important thread that links us to all of life. As Margulis humbly told science writer Jeanne McDermott, "All I ask is that we compare human consciousness with spirochete ecology." How strange to think that this thought you are thinking right now was launched by the twitch of a cell's tail!

From her studies in microbiology, Margulis has concluded that evolution does not always work for the good of the individual. "Just what is the 'individual' after all?" she asks. "Is it the 'single' amoeba with its internalized bacteria, or is it the 'single' bacterium living in the cellular environment which is itself alive? Really, the individual is something abstract, a category, a conception."

The human body that began with microscopic protists has come a long way, baby. Your physical existence has been millions of years in the making, growing through minuscule changes or sudden bursts of adaptation (punctuated equilibrium), producing refinements in eyes and jaw, limbs and lungs, propulsion and perception. Perhaps all of it was guided by some invisible "hand" or "intelligence" (human conceits) or a spirit that decided to work through the process of natural selection. Maybe evolution is simply the gods' way of remaining anonymous. Meanwhile, evolutionary theory suggests that there is no overarching plan, that life is not progressing, nor is nature going anywhere in particular.

Whether or not there is purpose or progress, the evidence that human beings did evolve from past life is now overwhelming, and through Buddhist meditations and reflections we can begin to integrate this understanding. By contemplating "the body as body" we can start to *feel* our connection with all life, our nature as nature. The following exercise—a variation on a classical Buddhist meditation—will guide us through the actual structure of our body. As we experience the architecture of our bones and tissues, we will simultaneously reflect on the latest scientific findings about the critical events in the biography of our body.

EXERCISE
<hr>

🐞 *A Veritable Vertebrate: A Guided Reflection* 🦋

> *The head bone's connected to the neck bone; the neck bone's connected to the shoulder bone; the shoulder bone's connected to the arm bone; the arm bone's connected to the hand bone . . .*
>
> TRADITIONAL SONG LYRIC

In this exercise we will be scanning our mindful attention down through the structure of our body. You might want to read through this entire reflection once to learn about some of the places of special evolutionary interest before actually attempting the body scan. If you then have some difficulty actually "feeling" the bones, let yourself visualize as you scan: follow the image of the human skeleton you have seen countless times in pictures or models. Another way to bring particular parts of your skeleton into focus is to move the bones around a little as you bring awareness to them.

The reflection can be done in any posture—seated, standing, or lying down. With your eyes closed, begin by bringing your attention to the very top of your head. Become aware of the rounded dome of the skull, sensing its weight, hardness, and shape.

Let your awareness move around the skull, noticing all of the empty spaces in the skull bone. Feel the openings: the eye sockets, the jaw and the cavity of the mouth, the space beneath the ears, and the big opening in the back of the skull where the spine enters.

You can feel all of these openings in the skull as the primary places where messages about the world come through. Isn't it convenient that the nose, eyes, ears, and mouth are so close to the brain? The rest of the body is still using a cable system, the spine, sending signals up and down the length of us.

To get an inward sense of the bones of the skull, just clench your jaw. Grind your teeth together a little. Don't set them on edge, just move them against each other. Feel the power in that finely wrought tool, your mouth—the jaws are perfectly crafted hinges. This tool can bite off vegetables or meat and chew them into a liquid if so directed. Your mouth, in spite of what may come out of it at times, is certainly one of the marvels of nature.

> *The invention of jaws . . . five hundred million years ago, may have given polychaete worms the advantage over priapulid worms. Hinged jaws were a turning point for armored fish, cartilaginous fish, and bony fish in the seas of the Paleozoic, and for the whole vertebrate evolution that followed, from amphibian to reptiles, birds, and mammals.*
>
> JONATHAN WEINER, *THE BEAK OF THE FINCH*

Once again, open your mouth and feel the jaw and the cavity of the throat. In the womb, we all develop gill-like structures just beneath our face, and after satisfying the DNA of primitive fish, these develop into jaws, ear bones, and larynx. Nature is a great recycler of characteristics. In fact, the skull inside your head is a refinement of the skull bones of countless other beings, designed by their suffering and triumphs. Your skull has been developing into this shape for a half billion years, expanding to accommodate a growing brain, slowly forming its narrow, brooding forehead.

Another way to feel the skull is to hum out loud, making a nasal sound that vibrates through the acoustic space in the dome of your head.

Visualize your skull. Recall some of the skulls and pictures of skulls you have seen—from museums, medical texts, Halloween, the Day of the Dead, the Grateful Dead; they are all reasonable facsimiles of the skull you are feeling inside your own face.

Before moving your attention away from your head, try to feel the entire skull as a single bone. Whenever you are "in your head," this is your living room. The skull is also holding your face in place; without it your head would cave in.

❧

Next move your attention downward and let it rest for a few minutes in your throat area. By taking a swallow or two you can feel the muscles on the inside of the throat and sense the relatively hard tissues of the esophagus. Next take a breath through your mouth, which allows you to feel or at least sense the air moving down into your trachea, the so-called windpipe.

Keeping your attention in the throat area, make a few sounds or say a few words out loud. The strongest sensations that you are likely to feel are from your vocal folds (cords) vibrating inside the larynx. Notice precisely where this vibration is located. The structure and placement of these small reeds of flesh is of vital importance in human evolution.

In most animals the larynx sits high in the throat and acts as a valve that can separate the trachea from the esophagus, allowing the animal to swallow and breathe at the same time. Human babies are born with the larynx high in the throat so that they too can breathe and drink simultaneously, but soon the larynx begins to migrate downward. Eventually the human larynx settles near the middle of the throat, leaving the space above it and at the back of the nose to act as a sound chamber, giving our voice a special resonance and allowing us to make a greater range of sounds. Add the extreme pliability of our tongue and lips, and you have the unique human ability to articulate *a, e, i, o, u,* and *y,* and all the consonants. This, in turn, allows us to communicate complicated ideas, to curse, coo, and sing. We can even imitate birds and other animals. We cannot, however, vocalize and eat or drink at the same time. It has been tried many times, often with embarrassing if not disastrous results.

Scientists agree that human speech has played a major role in our evolution. Large motor and sensory areas of our brains are dedicated to the lips, tongue, and pharynx, and thinkers such as MIT linguist Stephen Pinker believe that the brain increased in size as a result of the invention of language, rather than the other way around. As Richard Leakey has written, "The evolution of spoken language as we know it was a defining point in human prehistory. Perhaps it was the defining point."

Again, speak a few words, and this time feel the precisely coordinated movements of your tongue and lips. Notice how these take place automatically after you have decided which words you want to speak. Once again, speak a few words and feel the movement of your tongue, lips, and mouth, as well as the vibrations in your throat. What a piece of work we are!

Before you become too swollen with pride—human chauvinism—you might consider that many other species of life have developed equally remarkable and successful means of survival. As Stephen Jay Gould asks:

Do you prefer a marlin for its excellent spike; a flounder for its superb camouflage; an anglerfish for its peculiar "lure" evolved at the end of its own dorsal fin ray; a seahorse for its wondrous shape, so well adapted for bobbing around its habitat? Could any of these fishes be judged "better" or "more progressive" than any other? The question makes no sense. Natural selection can forge only local adaptation, wondrously intricate in some cases, but always local and not a step in a series of general progress or complexification.

Now continue to move your mindful awareness downward, into the bones of your neck, the topmost part of your spine. It is easiest to feel the spine as it rises through the thinness of the neck area. To experience both the flexibility and the firmness of these neck bones, try turning your head to the sides or up and down.

Next move the scan downward into the spine. Feel the central position of this axis of your body world. By arching your back and head or turning your body to the sides and back again you can feel the spine's fine engineering. If you sit up straight or stand and then let all the muscles of your upper body go slack, you will feel the strength of this great ridgepole holding you erect.

Our spine and ribs were born in the ocean, as tubular-shaped marine creatures began to develop ridges that segmented their body, along with a flexible spinal rod called a notochord. The structure was a way to protect the innards while still allowing for mobility. Five hundred million years ago these "chordates" gave rise to the first vertebrates, which were primitive fish. (Watch out for the bones!) Later these fish evolved into amphibians, and later reptiles and mammals. And we still carry the basic design, head to toes. (In scientific lingo, humans belong to the phylum of Chordates, which includes sea lemons, salamanders, and, I'm reluctant to admit, pigeons.)

After gaining a sense of the spine and rib cage, move your awareness into your shoulders and out through your arm bones. Move your arms around a little, feeling the range of motion and the precision of the engineering. Shrug the shoulders and flex the elbows, experiencing the hinges, the lever and fulcrum. These are the equivalent of fins, wings, or forelegs, once used for locomotion, now evolved into human arms and used for moving the world around, digging, lifting, rearranging the furniture. Sometimes for hugging.

Humans have uniquely versatile shoulders and wrists that can move through almost all the points of a circle or sphere. This mobility and dexterity is thought to be the gift of our brachiating ancestors, primates that swung from one tree branch to another. Their later transition from woodland to grass plain or savannah finally released the arms and hands from any work in locomotion. Instead they became tools for carrying things and for making other tools.

❧

Now move your conscious awareness into your hands, one of the great wonders of natural adaptation. Flex the wrist, move the fingers around, and, finally, wiggle the thumb. The incredible opposable thumb!

Play with this thumb for a few minutes. Press it against each of the other fingers. Then reach out and take hold of your knee or your other arm, or else the rim of a chair or the edge of a rug or blanket, using the full leverage of your thumb and four fingers. Then make your thumb immobile, either by folding it into your palm or by holding it away from the rest of your hand. Now try to take hold of something without the use of your thumb. It is so much harder getting an exacting grip on things! (As a fascinating, yet frustrating experiment, spend a half hour or fifteen minutes of your daily life with both thumbs immobilized. Just try buttoning your shirt.)

The limbs of all vertebrates begin in the womb as fin-like buds. For most mammals, the fin buds will turn into limbs, and the bone cartilage at the extremities of the limbs will grow five digits. For many animals, such as pigs, chickens, and horses, a few of those digits will disappear by birth.

> We owe the five fingers on our hands not to novel evolutionary events a million years ago on the African savannahs, but rather as a holdover from the original complement of five digits on the forefoot of the earliest land vertebrates (tetrapods) who evolved some 370 million years ago.
>
> LYNN MARGULIS AND DORIAN FAGAN, WHAT IS LIFE?

Maybe those tetrapods were growing digits just to hold on to land so that they wouldn't slip back into the sea. Hands have since become so dexterous that they can build rockets and computers that get us to the moon and back. They also can tie shoes, and some of them can even play the piano.

Take your hand. Maybe it is holding this book while your other hand is picking up a piece of toast or holding a cup, or even counting beads on a rosary or mala. You are ambidextrous. And your wiggly, triple-jointed fingers and extremely flexible wrist are part of the wonder. It's taken a half billion years to get your hand in this great shape.

> An intelligent octopus would probably regard eight arms as superior.
>
> STEPHEN JAY GOULD, FULL HOUSE

Of course, we are very proud of our hands because we possess an opposable thumb. But perhaps we are just now beginning to develop this five-appendage tool. Maybe someday our pinky finger will become as articulated as our thumb. Then we might be able to do even more things at the same time.

Now move your awareness down into your pelvic bone, the great pedestal of your body. This is the platform—a turning tabletop—upon which the entire top half of your body is resting. In many forms of martial arts, all movements start in the pelvis; it is the place where we center and stabilize ourselves.

Next move your awareness down into the two branches of your legs. Just as you did with the arms, move the parts of your legs around a little and feel their size, solidity, flexibility, and function. Feel the great thigh bone moving in the socket of the pelvis, and then the knee and ankle joints. These legs played a major role in the evolutionary history of our body. They enabled us to stand up and be counted.

Those who study evolution say that the actual human story begins in the African savannah, when our earliest ancestors switched from brachiation—swinging from one tree branch to another—to walking on the ground. That particular move, from the trees to the grasslands, required several major adaptations, including the behavior of rearing up and walking on two legs. Paleontologist Richard Leakey called standing up one of the most striking shifts in anatomy in all of evolution.

Standing up must have been traumatic. All of a sudden our genitalia were right out in front for everyone to see. We can assume that the wearing of a fig leaf or loincloth came into fashion soon after that.

Perhaps just as modesty arose from the lifting up of our bodies, pride may have arisen from the lifting up of our heads. As we became more physically removed from the Earth, we may have also become more psychologically remote.

Humans are now better than most other species at standing on two legs. Birds do it, and bears sometimes do it, and dogs can be taught to do it for a few minutes for a reward, but humans are perhaps the champions of bipedal locomotion. To the other animals, we two-legged humans must look like a circus act.

After we were walking upright for a couple of million years, maybe just getting used to the posture, all of a sudden our skulls started expanding. You would guess that standing up would have had the opposite effect, and that our feet would have become swollen instead. It turns out that the skull was expanding to make more room for a bigger brain. But that is a whole other story that we will save for later.

Man is a biped without feathers.

PLATO

Continue the skeletal scan by moving awareness down through your ankles and into your toes. Flex your toes; as you do, remember that not so long ago our ancestors used to hold on to branches and vines with those appendages. When you are brachiating around in the treetops you need to have a good toehold.

Let your awareness sink into the bones of your feet. This is your base, your bottom line, your place to take a stand. This is where you and the Earth most often meet.

You might want to do this vertebrate meditation occasionally, or even make it part of a regular meditation routine. Students report to me that even a few skeletal scans give them a new sense of the evolved nature of their body, and a subtle shift in their sense of identity.

You can also practice this vertebrate meditation while standing up, moving around, or walking, all of which will offer a whole different sense of your skeletal structure. When standing, find a stable position with your legs placed shoulder-width apart. Experience the trunk of bone rising up, with bone limbs extending out from it and the little bone twigs extending out from the limbs, all of it anchored but still capable of bending and moving in response to a wind blowing through. Let yourself bend the knees, move the arms and legs around, bend over and feel the spine, all the while being aware of the bones in motion.

Do a walk, just focusing your attention on the entire skeleton moving. Feel both the solidity and flexibility of this amazing structure. The Earth has come to life inside you. You are earth walking on Earth.

> *The eye bone's connected to the air bone, the air bone's connected to the sky bone, sky bone's connected to the angel bone, angel bone's connected to the god bone, the god bone's connected to the bone bone . . .*
>
> JACK KEROUAC, *VISIONS OF CODY*

DIE BEFORE YOU DIE

As we come to know our bodies as part of biological evolution and subject to natural processes, we eventually must face the fact of our physical death. No matter how tragic it may appear to us, it is nonetheless only natural.

The Buddha placed great importance on the contemplation of death, understanding that this practice has the power to awaken us like nothing else. Meditating on death brings us face-to-face with those characteristics of existence that we mostly try to avoid—the impermanence of all things, the inevitable suffering of conditioned beings, and the impersonality of the natural processes that govern all life.

The Buddha includes his contemplations of death under the First Foundation of Mindfulness, which focuses on the body, perhaps because no matter what one believes about the soul or consciousness living on, the body you now call yours will most certainly lose its life.

> *Animals—all with two-parent sex and fertilized eggs that form embryos—mature into reproductives that are subject to individually programmed death.*
> LYNN MARGULIS AND DORION SAGAN, *WHAT IS LIFE?*

Why do we die? While the metaphysical answer eludes us, scientists may be getting closer to the essential biological reasons. It turns out that the very cells that gave us life can also be blamed for our death.

Unlike humans, not all organisms age and die at the end of a regular time period. Some bacteria, for instance, do not die unless they are killed. According to Lynn Margulis, the aging and dying process, or "programmed death," is a product of evolution, first appearing in those innovative microbial ancestors, the protists.

As explained earlier, the protists are formed by the merging of different cells through the process of symbiogenesis. One type of cell making up the new organism has the ability to divide (mitosis) and create two versions of itself. Another type of cell—the whiplashing spirochete—has the ability to form tails or cilia (undulipodia, or "waving feet") and becomes expert in propulsion, in sensing and discriminating among environmental stimuli, and in gathering and moving food and water through the organism's system. However, because this second type of animal cell has dedicated its energy to forming undulipodial shafts, it no longer has the capacity for mitotic cell division. It can no longer reproduce itself.

By sticking together, the two types of animal cells were able to do great things, such as evolve into human beings. However, according to Margulis, "Our animal ancestors never solved the problem of 'How can I divide and at the same time swim by means of undulipodia?'" As a solution, the protists evolved a two-cell system of reproduction. That way they could keep the advantages gained by growing undulipodia, and still be able to pass on their DNA. But the upshot is that this solution also brings with it the legacy of death. The animal organism they formed cannot divide itself and maintain eternal youth but must instead get its DNA into a separate body and then eventually grow old and die. In exchange for our complexity, we must accept our mortality.

If I had an option, I think I would rather divide than die. Although it is traumatic to imagine losing one half of myself, I could also think of it as a way of doubling my chances for a happy life. Furthermore, since cell division is an alternative to sexual reproduction, dividing may feel similar to having sex. Perhaps we could even call the process of dividing "love." I'm sure we could work it out, but alas, Nature has chosen for us death.

Among all the animals, humans seem to be the only ones with foreknowledge of our own death. It comes in the small print at the bottom of our lease on life. Although this knowledge sometimes feels like a curse, it can be understood as a great gift. Unlike with the other animals, Nature is at least offering us humans a little time to get comfortable with the idea of death and to see if we can learn something from it—before Nature kills us, one by one.

Ever since we got wind of our own death, we have been trying to find ways to escape it, either through immortality potions and open-heart surgeries, or through religious belief in reincarnation or some kind of afterlife. What if we stopped trying to escape and instead learned to embrace our death?

In the *Phaedo,* Plato writes that the "true votaries of knowledge . . . practice nothing else but how to die or meet death." As the Zen masters say, "Die before you die." Then maybe when you die you won't have to die. At the last moment you can say to death, "Been there. Done that."

The advice is that we step into our death. Try it on for size. Get comfortable wearing it. Practice death every day, or at least once a week. As one of my meditation students once said, as a take-off on a political election slogan, "Die early and often."

Consider that if we do have many lives—a common belief in several parts of the world—then we must also have many deaths, so we might as well practice dying and get good at it. Also, the sages say that only by learning how to die do we finally learn how to live. Such a deal—two lessons in one!

But there's a catch. Many of those sages will also tell you that once you have learned how to die, and hence how to live, you finally are free of the wheel of rebirths; you will not be born again. In other words, just when you get it right the journey is over! Oh, well. That's life.

Making Friends with Death

Of all the footprints, that of the elephant is supreme. Similarly, of all mindfulness meditations, that on death is supreme.

THE BUDDHA, *THE PARINIRVANA SUTRA*

As an aid in contemplating physical death, the Buddha recommends that his followers go to a charnel ground to view the bodies waiting to be burned, or those that have been discarded and are in one stage or another of decomposition. The instructions read, "If a monk sees a body one day dead, or two days dead, or three days dead, swollen, blue, and festering, discarded in the charnel ground, he then applies [this perception] to his own body thus: 'Truly, this body of mine too is of the same nature; it will become like that and will not escape from it.'" The monks are then advised to look around the charnel ground for bodies that might be in further stages of decay, and to acknowledge that "this body of mine too is of the same nature." You probably don't have a charnel ground to go to in your vicinity, but the progressive disintegration of the body is graphically described in the *Mahasatipatthana Sutra*; except for a few specific details, the description can be used as a rough guide to visualizing the fate of *anybody* after death.

If a monk sees a body discarded in the charnel ground being devoured by crows, hawks, vultures, herons, dogs, leopards, tigers, jackals, or by various kinds of worms . . . [or] reduced to a skeleton held together by the tendons, with some flesh and blood adhering to it . . . [or] a fleshless skeleton smeared with blood and held together by the tendons . . . [or] a skeleton without flesh and blood held together by tendons . . . [or] reduced to loose bones scattered in all directions—here a hand bone, there bones of the foot, shin bones, thigh bones, pelvis, spine, and skull . . . bones bleached white to a shell-like color . . . bones more than a year old lying in a heap . . . decomposed bones, crumbling to powder . . . he applies this perception to his own body thus: "Truly, this body of mine too is of the same nature; it will become like that and will not escape from it."

The Buddha does not let us pull back from this truth. He holds our gaze on the decomposing body to show us that Nature will have its way with us, no matter how smart we think we are. Contemplation of death reminds us that our life is part of an organic process that goes on without our advice or consent.

Since the Buddha's time, many different ways of meditating on death have been devised in Buddhist communities. In their religious rituals, Tibetan Buddhist monks blow ceremonial horns made of human bones, and they sometimes eat their meals out of bowls made from human skulls. In the temples and monasteries of Thailand, one will often find pictures of skeletons hanging on the wall. They might depict, for example, a middle-class family—father, mother, and child— with half of each body clothed and face smiling, while the other half is a bare-boned skeleton.

In some sense, the act of mindfulness meditation itself could be understood as a practice of dying—to each moment. If you get good at it, your last moment will be easier. Mindfulness meditation can also be thought of as learning to let go of the ideas we have about ourselves, and those may be all that are holding us together in the first place.

Contrary to what most people might believe, meditation on death is not about morbidity or denying of life. Many meditators report that contemplating death brings them a renewed appreciation for being alive. Suddenly, this very breath can seem to be enough. After reflecting on death, one's life needs no other justification than itself.

When death comes to find you, may it find you alive.
AFRICAN SAYING

As you reflect on death, you might acknowledge that it is not only you who dies, but everybody and everything. Death happens to people, cities, civilizations, knowledge, and fashions, even planets and world systems. Scientists believe the universe itself will either die in what's known as a "cold death," thinning out into nothingness, or in a "big crunch" collapsing into a very dense point or singularity. Which do you prefer?

When you contemplate your personal death you might also consider that from the perspective of quantum physics, there is no such thing as death. Matter-energy continues to dance on through space-time, moving to its own rhythms, oblivious to whether we call it one thing or another. Everything is alive and continues to live, whether it has your name on it or not. However, that knowledge may not be much consolation, especially if you are very attached to your current name and form.

> *Nothing is ever at rest—wood, iron, water, everything is alive, everything is raging, whirling, whizzing, day and night and night and day, nothing is dead, there is no such thing as death, everything is full of bristling life, tremendous life, even the bones of the crusader that perished before Jerusalem eight centuries ago.*
>
> MARK TWAIN, *THREE THOUSAND YEARS AMONG THE MICROBES*

Each of us humans goes from womb to world to tomb, and, some would say, back to start again. Every ending is also a beginning, and death must lead someplace, perhaps back to life. And, of course, we know that without death for a comparison there would be no such thing as life. Death is indeed one of our best friends. And with friends like death, who needs enemies?

EXERCISE

☙ Not to Be: Death Reflection ☙

Without being mindful of death, whatever Dharma practices you take up will be merely superficial.

MILAREPA, *THE ONE HUNDRED THOUSAND SONGS OF MILAREPA*

Close your eyes and bring your attention inward. First establish mindfulness of your body, becoming aware of its shape and weight, its warmth and vitality.

Bring consciousness to the pulses of your breath and heartbeat, one pulse gathering in energy and the other pulse pumping it throughout your body. Be aware of your strength, and that you can hold your body erect as a result of these pulses.

Next, take a few minutes to become aware of your current state of mind. Check in on your mood and your thoughts. Are you curious, anxious, impatient, contented? Remember that death may come to you in an ordinary living moment, just like this one. Wouldn't it be ironic if you were making some long-term plans or worrying over some trivial pursuit?

Now begin to imagine that you are in the final process of your dying. Sense that the muscle of your heart is weakening and beginning to slow down. Imagine that in a few minutes your heart will quit beating, your blood will stop circulating, and due to a lack of oxygen and other nutrients your flesh will begin to grow weak. Imagine your entire body growing heavy and lifeless. Meanwhile, your mind, having recognized death at the last minute, will probably be running quickly through scenes from your life, an experience that those who have survived describe as rather chaotic. Finally, all the thoughts and images will begin to disappear like a fading radio dimming out into static and white noise.

As you imagine your death, what feelings arise? Is there an alarm going off in your chest? A systems alert lighting up in your head? If you can truly imagine your death, chances are you will begin to hear some strong signals. Your survival brain speaks loudest when death is hanging around.

It is quite possible that when you imagine the death of your body you will feel deep sorrow or fear. Whatever emotion arises, let it be there in mindful awareness for a few minutes. Let the feeling become as strong as it wants to be, even exaggerate it if you wish. To reactivate this feeling or to make it stronger, once again imagine your body dying.

Bring your awareness back to your breath for a few minutes to reestablish mindfulness. Then turn your attention to your current plans, concerns, desires—the issues of your life at this particular time. Then again return to the feeling that in a few minutes you will die. All of this mental life that you call yours will disappear—all the thoughts, political opinions, financial schemes, jealousies and vendettas, regrets and sorrows, everything you had to get done this week—feel all of that floating away into nothingness. When your body dies, so will your mental life.

Does the fear return? What other emotion accompanies the imagining of your own death? Regret for things not done, life not completed? Experience these feelings, hold them, let them grow, explore them.

You may want to do death meditation lying down. Then you can let your body go limp, sinking into the floor or ground. You can even imagine that you are on your deathbed or in a coffin.

If you happen to feel a sense of happiness or relief during the death meditation, it doesn't mean you are a self-loathing individual. In fact, as a separate reflection you might even try looking at the upbeat or brighter side of death.

Once again, establish mindfulness and imagine your body dying, only this time realize that after death you no longer will have to struggle with gravity. You will no longer have to work in order to pay for shelter or to feed and fuel this particular form.

What a deep rest it will be! No longer do you have to react to the stimuli of the world (at least not in this form or this world). Furthermore, the demands of your needy, vulnerable, and all-too-human personality will be ended. You won't have to satisfy it with special experiences, or struggle to make it happy. You will get to take a long rest from reacting to yourself. Although no one knows for sure what happens after death, some reports of near-death experiences describe it as delicious peace. Maybe we have nothing to fear from death but nothing—and nothing is the best thing that ever happens to us.

Death is just infinity closing in.

JORGE LUIS BORGES

Before you bring an end to any of the death reflections, be sure to return your awareness to the breath and heartbeat, at least for a few minutes. Once again experience the pulses of life. Feel the warmth of your body telling you that metabolism is continuing; feel the strength of your muscles and flesh, your ability to hold yourself erect and move your limbs. Feel yourself come back to life.

Last Words

In Japan, a tradition among Zen monks, samurai warriors, and artists is to write a "death poem" as one approaches the final moments of life. It is cheating for someone to write a death poem too early, since the poem will be a testament to one's level of spiritual attainment when looking death directly in the face. On their deathbeds, the greatest of sages will be fearless, and ready with wry and enlightened perceptions. Here are a few examples taken from an excellent compilation and study by Yoel Hoffmann entitled *Japanese Death Poems*.

> *My old body:*
> *a drop of dew grown*
> *heavy at the leaf tip.*
>
> KIBA

> *Till now I thought that*
> *death befell*
> *the untalented alone.*
> *If those with talent, too,*
> *must die*
> *surely they make*
> *a better manure?*
>
> KYORIKU

Though I should live
To be a hundred,
The same world, the same
    cherry-blossoms:
The moon is round,
The snow is white.

TAIYA TEIRYU

A few days before his death, Zen teacher Kozan Ichikyo called his pupils together and ordered them to bury him without ceremony, even forbidding them to hold services in his memory. He wrote this poem on the morning of his death, laid down his brush, and died sitting upright.

Empty-handed I entered the world
Barefoot I leave it.
My coming, my going—
Two simple happenings
That got entangled.

It is customary and auspicious for Zen monks to die while sitting up, in meditation. Chinese Zen master Chihhsien asked his disciples, "Who dies sitting?" They answered, "A monk." Then he asked, "Who dies standing?" His disciples answered, "Enlightened monks." Chihhsien then took seven steps and died standing up.

Meanwhile, Zen monk Teng Yinfeng asked his followers if anyone had ever died upside down. When they told him it had never been seen or heard of, Teng stood on his head and died. A great closing act.

CHAPTER FIVE

❯❯❯ ❮❮❮

The Second Foundation of Mindfulness

The First Impression

For some people, contact, the point where sense plus object meet, is enthralling. And so they are washed by the tides of being, drifting along an empty, pointless road. But others come to understand their sense activity, and because they understand it, the stillness fills them with delight.

THE BUDDHA, *SUTTA NIPATA*

The Second Foundation of Mindfulness, and the next stop on our evolutionary journey, is feelings, *vedana* in Sanskrit. These are not emotions, which are generally considered more complex and subtle, but rather the simplest feelings of pleasant, unpleasant, or neutral, the basic sense impressions. We are now moving our awareness from the physical body to the nervous system—from elements, organs, and bones into the beginning of the sensing process by which we contact and interpret the world.

The Buddha devotes an entire foundation of mindfulness to basic sense impressions because this is the place where our experience begins.

Here we will discover what we inherit from all of life—the instinctual movements of approach-avoidance, fight or flight. Here we can see the beginning of biologically conditioned desire, lust, fear, and hatred. Freud called them drives or instincts, and they are commonly known as *animal* instincts.

The Buddha called them "underlying tendencies." In Buddhist texts these underlying tendencies are qualities that we are born with and that have their origin in the unknowable distant past. What the Buddha understood is really *very* simple: as sentient beings we have a nervous system that works according to principles of stimulus-response. If we experience a pleasant sensation, we automatically want more of the same, and when we experience a painful sensation, we want it to go away. We move toward the things that feel good or that feed us, and away from things that feel uncomfortable or threaten our survival. These built-in reactions are common to all sentient beings. Even a single cell retracts its membrane when it bumps into something unpleasant and extends it when there is food in the vicinity.

Although these reactions are perfectly natural, if we remain unconscious of them we have no freedom at all; we are totally at the mercy of our evolutionary karma. As the old accusation claims, we are "no different from an animal," and, for that matter, no different from a bacterium. This is not to imply that we should somehow be better or "above" the other forms of life, but the Buddha realized that we do have the potential to respond differently to these hardwired instincts, and that it would serve us well to exercise and develop this potential.

The Buddha's instructions in the *Mahasatipatthana Sutra* for the Second Foundation of Mindfulness are quite simple. "When experiencing a pleasant feeling, the meditator knows: 'I experience a pleasant feeling'; when experiencing a painful feeling, the meditator knows: 'I experience a painful feeling'; when experiencing a neutral feeling, the meditator knows: 'I experience a neutral feeling.'"

The Buddha is trying to draw our mindful attention to these basic sensations so that we can begin to see how they trigger our instincts. He wants us to witness, up close and personal, how automatic reactions to sense impressions keep us caught in a continuous push and pull struggle with the world. He especially wants us to see how this primal conditioning is dragging us into unchosen and dissatisfied states of mind.

In the *Chachakka Sutra,* the Buddha takes us through each of our senses, one at a time, and explains how the conditioning works. Using a moment of seeing, for example, the Buddha says, "Dependent on the eye and forms, eye-consciousness arises; the meeting of these three is contact; with contact as condition there is feeling (pleasant, unpleasant, or neutral); with feeling as condition there is craving [or aversion]." He is pointing out that because of underlying tendencies our feelings of pleasant or unpleasant will invariably turn into mental states of craving or aversion.

We usually become conscious of this sequence, if at all, only after the craving or aversion has begun. Until then our primal conditioning is completely in charge, dragging us into emotions or behavior we may not have chosen, had we been aware of their origin. For that reason, the Buddha advises us to practice bringing awareness to basic sense impressions, the starting point of our mind-states and emotions.

The Buddha's instructions for this meditation practice may at first sound outlandish: "One shall here and now make an end of suffering by abandoning the underlying tendency to lust for pleasant feeling, and by abolishing the underlying tendency to aversion toward painful feeling."

Who in his or her right mind would want to abandon the desire for pleasant feelings and the aversion for unpleasant ones? Perhaps a sadomasochist. This instruction sounds like it could lead only to a complete alienation from the body, a literal "taking leave of one's senses."

But the Buddha is not saying that we should try to avoid pleasure, and certainly not suggesting that we seek pain. (He went through his own physical austerities, such as fasting almost to the death, and then rejected such practices as unnecessary for awakening.) What the Buddha is advising us to do is to become aware of our *automatic reactions* to pleasure and pain. When we see that we are not choosing these reactions we will no longer be so bound by their commands. We may then begin to experience a different kind of satisfaction that comes from more freedom and ease of mind.

Therefore, while the meditation on sensations may sound counter-intuitive, it can more accurately be described as *counter-instinctive*. We are training our mind to notice the knee-jerk reactions. We are learning how to recognize our evolutionary karma and, in the process, loosening some of its hold over us. We have been given this ability by Nature, and the Buddha discovered how to use it well.

Although biologists and Freudian psychologists may consider it unrealistic to challenge our instincts, the Buddha often says to his followers, "this is possible." And he assures us that when the underlying tendencies are no longer completely in charge, "One's bodily and mental troubles are abandoned, one's bodily and mental torments are abandoned, one's bodily and mental fevers are abandoned, and one experiences bodily and mental pleasure."

THE BIRTH OF THE BRAIN

> *If we choose to let conjecture run wild, then animals, our fellow brethren in pain, disease, suffering and famine— our companions in our amusements—they may partake of our origin in one common ancestor—we may all be netted together."*
>
> CHARLES DARWIN, QUOTED IN
> LOREN EISELEY, *STAR THROWER*

If the Buddha were alive today, I am certain he would want us to read and reflect on what science tells us about the human brain and nervous system. The more we understand about how our thoughts and behaviors are generated, the more capable we will be of creating contentment for ourselves and others.

In particular, the Buddha would be interested in the neuroscientists' view of how the brain evolved, and their organic explanation of our instincts or underlying tendencies. The latest brain research sheds new light on why humans often seem to be out of control, acting like beasts or monsters, frequently against their own best interests and happiness. This problem was a primary concern of the Buddha.

Neuroscientist Paul MacLean devoted his life to exploring the brain's development. After years of research at the National Institute of Mental Health's Laboratory of Brain Evolution and Behavior, MacLean came to the startling conclusion that human beings don't really have *a* brain. We have *three* brains in one, what MacLean called a triune brain.

MacLean discovered that within our skull resides what he described as a reptilian brain, a mammalian brain, and the cerebral cortex, or primate brain—also known as the reptilian, paleomammalian, and neomammalian brains. Even more startling is the fact that all three of these brains take part in creating our reality, which means that there's still a little lizard and lemur in all of us.

MacLean recognized that just as in the evolution of species, these three brains develop sequentially as we grow inside our mother's womb. First is the reptilian brain, based in a structure called the brain stem located at the top of the spine. The reptilian brain regulates functions such as breath, body temperature, pain perception, hunger, sexuality, and a basic nervous system program of stimulus-response.

In our evolutionary journey through the Four Foundations of Mindfulness, we can follow MacLean's description of the brain as triune. The activities of the reptilian brain correspond roughly to the Second Foundation of Mindfulness ("arising"). This brain region is hardwired to react to basic feelings of pleasant or unpleasant, with little flexibility. Reptiles probably do not have behavioral options, and probably don't care. As Jon Franklin wrote in his Pulitzer Prize–winning book *Molecules of the Mind,* "Such a creature is a puppet on an evolutionary string."

Sometime in the distant past, a more elaborate brain system began to develop in mammals, starting with new layers of cells that grew around the rim of the brain stem. Scientists consider this structure to be part of the emotional brain, named the limbic system by MacLean, from the Latin *limbus,* meaning "rim." It is also commonly known as the visceral or mammalian brain.

The mammalian brain operates over a complex web of interconnected brain cells, providing an increased ability to respond in unique ways to changing circumstances. With increased powers of learning and memory, a mammal doesn't have to make the same mistake twice, at least not forever. A smell can be compared to past smells, for instance, and food that has gone bad will be avoided, along with the painful experience of trying to digest it.

The mammalian brain generates emotions. The sexual drive of the lizard begins to shade into more elaborate feelings and behavior, such as loyalty and affection. The lizard's reactions to predator or prey become more nuanced in the mammalian brain. If the bear is gorging on blueberries, you might just give it a wide berth, but if you suddenly come upon it walking with its cubs you will run away as fast as possible. With the limbic system, degrees of danger and opportunity can be ascertained.

Although the mammalian brain grew over the top of the reptilian brain, it did not assume complete control. MacLean emphasized that the mammalian brain is tightly connected to the reptilian circuits and can function only within their constraints. Although our reptilian ancestors are in the distant past, the lizard inside us still has some say over the behavior of the lemur. As the Buddha pointed out in his teaching, it is our primal reaction to feelings of pleasant or unpleasant that draws us into emotional states of craving or aversion.

The third brain system to develop in each human embryo is known as the neomammalian or primate brain. Here, the neocortex has greatly expanded, adding many more layers of cells. The brain has been remodeled from a small house to an estate, full of amazing new rooms, corridors, and even suites. The primate brain offers its user more options, an expanded power to learn and remember, and a new sense of agency and individuality.

As if that weren't enough—and it must not have been—a few million years ago, in one of the fastest evolutionary adaptations ever, the neocortex suddenly began adding many additional groups of cells, especially in the region of the prefrontal lobes. This expansion of the primate brain brought with it a completely new way of seeing and being. It was as if life had been hit by lightning a second time, as human beings leapt away from all ancestors, with complex language, long-term planning ability, abstract thought, and a very strong sense of individuality and control over the world. We are now looking at the Buddha's Fourth Foundation of Mindfulness (the "path"), which are the complex functions known as the mind.

It is significant that in the Buddha's teaching, the cognitive mind is often mentioned as a sixth sense organ. The Buddha regarded thinking as one of the natural, evolved processes that we can experience as human beings, but an attribute that is not so different in kind from our other sensing abilities. His perspective is unique in premodern cultures but is currently being embraced by modern science.

As MacLean himself realized, there are drawbacks to this model of the brain; for example, there is considerable anatomic overlap among the three brain regions, the flow of information is not necessarily from top down, and the evolutionary development of the three layers is complex. However, as Robert Sapolsky points out in *Behave: The Biology of Humans at our Best and Worst,* the triune model is "a good organizing metaphor" for understanding the brain.

Although you may imagine that three brains are better than one,

Jon Franklin reminds us: "Each of us today, be we garbage collector, teacher, police officer, preacher, or president, must march to the tune of three different drummers. And so each of our thoughts, before we are allowed to think it, must meet the approval of a cold-blooded, scaly thing that nestles at the psychic crossroads in the center of our brain."

We fail and perhaps are loath to acknowledge that our brain and central nervous system are one part "cold-blooded, scaly thing." We also don't want to admit that we are one part fabulous furry freak brother. Yet the overwhelming evidence indicates that much of our thought, feeling, and behavior has its roots in other forms of life, and in the far-distant past.

One early offshoot of the triune brain theory claims—and many people would like to believe—that the architecture of our three brains is a key to our psychology, with the primal brain stem on the bottom, the limbic system on top of that, and the cerebral cortex like a cap on top of the others. According to this theory, the top brain is holding down the reptilian and animal instincts of the other two brains. The top brain is seen as a lid on the id. While there may be some truth to that idea, psychologist and author Joseph Chilton Pearce speculates that, for now anyway, we are using the most human part of our brain to make excuses for the behavior generated by our reptilian and mammalian brains. We like to think of ourselves as very different from reptiles and other mammals, so we get embarrassed when we act like them.

Since MacLean's discovery, neuroscientists have uncovered a more nuanced understanding of the evolutionary brain. We now know that no brain region is unique to humans. It's not that the human brain became more complex *in terms of its basic plan*; it only became more human. There was no superseding of a less complex brain by a more complex one; all animal life has had a shared blueprint of brains for over half a billion years. We aren't more complex, we're just more human, and we can realize our Buddha Nature through embracing that humanness and *its roots in nonhumanness.*

Some neuroscientists believe that we're still not using the full capacity of our brains. Perhaps evolution is planning ahead and the not-yet-used capacity means that we're just in transition to another level of consciousness. There's no reason to believe that creation is done or that humanity is a finished product. At this very moment, natural selection is busy selecting for traits. Nothing in nature is fixed; all species are in jittery motion. So, at this moment we are a missing link, and most likely missing a link or two. The Buddha would no doubt agree with that assessment, and as proof might point to the mostly underdeveloped faculty of mindfulness.

According to the Buddha's teaching, we can do much more with our new brain capacity. Through meditations on the Second Foundation of Mindfulness ("arising"), each of us can learn how our lizard and lemur ancestors are pushing us around. Once we see the evolutionary origin of our desires and fears, we are no longer so driven by them, not so lost in their dramas. We gain evolutionary wisdom and start to experience a new degree of peace and freedom of mind.

> *Meditation is about seeing the ape instinct of ego.*
> CHOGYAM TRUNGPA

THE ONE TASTE

> *A meditator looks at his or her senses and understands how the senses work, both in the mind and in the outside world. The meditator sees with clarity, goes beyond "black and white," and is steadfast.*
> THE BUDDHA, SUTTA NIPATA

For the first few years that I studied Buddhism, I practiced a meditation technique that focused on sense impressions, the Second Foundation of Mindfulness. I began this practice in India in 1970, under the guidance of S. N. Goenka.

After I had been practicing for several months, one day Goenka called me into his room, ostensibly inviting me to eat lunch with him. It turned out that he did not want to chat with me over a meal, but rather to lead me through a guided meditation on the sensations of eating.

First, he had me serve myself from a table of food—curried potatoes and carrots, almond rice, mango and orange chutneys, savory dahl. After I had put all of these delicacies into a single bowl, Goenka told me to close my eyes and reach into the bowl and just feel the food, its texture, temperature, degree of moistness. I was told to keep my focus on the basic sensations and my reactions to them.

First of all, because I was culturally unaccustomed to having mushy, slippery foodstuffs in my hand, the sensations were unpleasant to me. As I moved my hand around in the bowl the hunger for taste, which had been strongly aroused when I saw the food, quickly began to diminish. Along with the feel of it, I also don't think I liked the idea of the food all mashed together. After I placed the food into my mouth (eyes still closed), I was instructed to just hold it there without chewing, and to experience my elemental sensations and reactions. What I felt was the consistency and touch of the food on my palate, the moisture released into my mouth by my salivary glands, and some slight variations in the temperature of the food.

As soon as the food touched my tongue, however, I no longer had any aversion to the feel of it. Now I only wanted to taste, chew, and swallow it. In fact, simply holding the food in my mouth for several minutes was very difficult; my whole system was demanding, "Get on with it!"

Goenka then instructed me to begin chewing the food, being mindful of what occurred. As I bit down I could feel an explosion of sensations on my tongue, followed a split second later by the recognition of the tastes of sweet, salty, and sour. Immediately after feeling those sensations, I experienced an avalanche of desire. My jaw immediately wanted to work faster, and I felt my tongue try to push the food toward the back of my mouth to make room for more bites and therefore more bursts of flavor. Even though the food was not thoroughly chewed, the impulse to swallow would also arise, motivated by the desire for the fresh taste that a new bite of food would bring.

For most of this eating meditation, it seemed as though my desire for taste was working in tandem with my stomach's desire for expansion and in sync with my entire system's desire for nutrients, all of them in chorus insisting, "Keep the food coming!" At some point, however, I could feel the demand for nutrient and stomach expansion slow down. I was feeling "full." But the desire for taste paid no attention to the feelings of my stomach. The highly sensitive tongue simply wanted to go on having its explosions of sensation, accustomed as it is to the intensities of flavor that keep us eating and therefore alive.

I must say that the curries were delicious—when I let myself taste them. But the taste of that particular meal was beside the point. Instead, I was shown how unconscious forces are guiding my behavior—at least three times a day. I also became aware of the interplay between hunger and taste: I understood that sensual desire is really the servant of survival. Perhaps for the first time in my life, I experienced the universal and impersonal quality of desire, and felt its origin in pleasant and unpleasant sensations. That meal added a new taste to my palate—what the Zen masters sometimes refer to as "the one taste"—and gave me a powerful lesson in evolutionary wisdom.

Through exercises such as the eating meditation, we become aware of the basic biological level of our experience, before any personal judgment, projection, or sentiment is added. The Buddha wants to demystify our life; he wants us to look beneath all the stories we tell ourselves so that their spell will be broken. He advised his followers to train themselves thoroughly in the Second Foundation of Mindfulness, so that, "in the seen, there will be just the seen, in the heard just the heard, in the sensed just the sensed."

YOU ARE NOT SOLID

Man generally makes the external world the object of his observations, and the more he becomes aware of the transitoriness of the world, the more he believes himself to be constant. If he would make himself the object of his analysis, soon the opportunity would arise to see his own impermanence.

ANAGARIKA GOVINDA, *THE PSYCHOLOGICAL ATTITUDE OF EARLY BUDDHIST PHILOSOPHY*

The primary technique that I used during my years of study with Goenka was called the body scan, a version of which was presented earlier in the exploration of the skeleton. The body scan that I originally practiced was focused on physical sensations and was partly used to reveal and integrate the truth of impermanence. The body scan method is sometimes referred to as "sweeping," and the cohort of American students studying alongside me with Goenka would joke that we were "sweeping our egos out the door."

The instructions were simple. We were told to close our eyes and move our mindful attention up and down our bodies from head to toe in a regular pattern, noticing any and all of the sensations we could feel. At first the sensations I felt were relatively solid or gross: I would notice hardness, heat, tension, some prickly or tingling sensations, but many areas of my body felt numb or vacant of any feeling at all. After several weeks of practice, however, I began to experience finer and more subtle sensations throughout my body. Eventually, after my mental concentration and mindfulness were more developed, I would scan through my body and feel no solidity at all, only a mass of minute, tingling sensations.

In the instructions for the Second Foundation of Mindfulness in the *Mahasatipatthana Sutra,* the Buddha tells his followers to contemplate the "origination" and "dissolution" of feelings. He wants us to absorb an awareness of the fleeting quality of all sensations. Then we will no longer become so entranced and controlled by them: we will realize that unpleasant sensations will not last and that, for the same reason, pleasant sensations cannot permanently satisfy us.

In my mind, I can still hear Goenka's voice, a booming baritone, intoning over and over—"*anicca, anicca, anicca . . . ,*" the Pali word for impermanence—as we moved our attention through our bodies. After a few months of training my mind to feel the subtle changes in bodily sensation I found that I was noticing the effervescent quality of sights, sounds, and thoughts as well. The body scan exercise began to teach me about the radical impermanence of all my experience.

Look around you for a few moments, or else close your eyes and become aware of your sense impressions or thoughts. Can you hold on to a single moment's perception? Can you freeze a thought, or stop a sound or physical sensation so that it does not change at all? It is impossible, of course, because all of reality is constantly in motion. Training yourself to see this impermanence as part of your *personal* reality—the fundamental nature of your own body, mind, and life experience— becomes a lesson in letting go.

Throughout the texts, over and over again the Buddha summarizes his teachings by saying, "Develop a mind that clings to nothing." When we realize that we can't hold on to a single moment of our experience, we begin to develop a mind that clings to nothing, because it has no other choice.

PAIN WITHOUT SUFFERING

Many people have probably seen pictures of yogis lying on a bed of nails. They are often pictured performing in a public place, a crowd gathered to witness this feat believed to demonstrate spiritual achievement. Their ability to lie on a bed of nails is not accomplished through any esoteric magic, or because of special rubber-tipped nails, but is primarily due to the fact that they have discovered how to become more comfortable with feelings of pain. One might even say they have learned not to take pain so personally.

A classical Buddhist text, the *Samyutta Nikaya,* describes two kinds of pain. The person with an untrained mind "when touched by painful bodily feelings, weeps and grieves and laments." This person "experiences both a bodily pain and a mental one. But one who has trained in mindfulness, when touched by a painful bodily feeling, does not weep, grieve, and lament. [That person] feels only one kind of pain."

In his book *Full Catastrophe Living,* Jon Kabat-Zinn explains how chronic pain patients experienced significant reductions in their levels of pain through a program that includes mindfulness meditation. At the Stress Reduction Clinic at the University of Massachusetts (UMass) Medical Center, Kabat-Zinn developed pioneering work exploring the uses of meditation in medicine and healing. One important aspect of this work applied the Buddha's Second Foundation of Mindfulness, focusing on the sensations of pain.

The attitude of mindfulness meditation toward pain is to get to know it and name it, and maybe even make friends with it. The first instruction for participants in pain management clinics is to begin to experience their pain, to *feel* the sensations, *allow* them, *explore* them. A key tool the participants are given is mindfulness, which can provide some space from habitual reactions to the sensations. Over the course of Kabat-Zinn's program, some participants experience such a radical shift in their relationship to their pain that they no longer use the word "pain" to describe it. What is being felt instead, they report, is simply very strong sensations.

Using a standard pain-rating index questionnaire, more than 61 percent of the patients in Kabat-Zinn's early clinic achieved at least a 50 percent reduction in their chronic pain, while 72 percent achieved at least a 33 percent reduction. In follow-up studies done up to four years after the patients had left the clinic, Kabat-Zinn discovered that the effects of the meditation program had been lasting. Most of the former participants were still meditating. They found it positively affected their lives in many ways, and their pain levels remained low. Similar results were reported for each group that completed Kabat-Zinn's eight-week program at the clinic.

What was happening in Kabat-Zinn's clinic was more than a medical technique. The participants were developing more ease with how they experienced and responded to pain, and also seeing into the ever-changing nature of sensation. One might even say there was a shifting of identity going on, that the participants began to take their experience of pain a bit less personally. What was once "my pain" had perhaps become simply "pain," a condition of being human.

Fast forward a few decades: Kabat-Zinn's original Stress Reduction Clinic is now the UMass Memorial Health Center for Mindfulness, and his Mindfulness-Based Stress Reduction (MBSR) program can be found in hospitals, universities, government agencies, and other organizations worldwide. Studies continue to come up showing the significant benefits of these programs on participants' well-being.

SITTING TILL IT HURTS

Some schools of meditation emphasize sitting for long periods of time in one posture without moving, partly as an unspoken way of offering the student the opportunity to meet pain in a controlled setting, and to examine its nature. If you sit long enough, almost invariably pain will show up.

Like many new practitioners, when I began to meditate I had a very difficult time getting into a comfortable seated position on my pillow on the floor. It was impossible for me to get into the traditional full lotus, with the legs folded up; around, and through each other like pretzels, and I struggled just to get into a relatively stable "half-lotus" that still left my knees wobbling above the floor.

After several months of meditation practice in India, during one intensive retreat Goenka guided his students to sit without moving for increasingly long periods of time. I worked up to taking vows not to change my bodily posture for up to two hours. And no matter how I tried to cushion my buttocks or my knees, after a while the pain would begin, often turning into the searing, burning variety. At that point, I could no longer focus my awareness on anything but the pain. Luckily that was what I was instructed to do when the pain arose: to focus mindfulness on the pain—to taste it, swim in it, burn with it—and also to explore my habitual reactivity to it.

I am not a martyr for enlightenment nor particularly heroic, but gradually I was able to sit with the pain for up to two hours. And the longer I sat with pain, the easier it became for me to experience it. I found that the feelings were continually changing, the so-called pain dissolving into a flowing stream of sensations, or becoming a deep pulse like a bass drumbeat, or a snaking, shivering series of twitches. As I came to understand that the pain was not solid nor constant, it was no longer so threatening.

Working with sensations of pain in meditation has given me a deep sense of confidence that I can manage the intense difficulties that life might have waiting for me, and also a newfound courage.

As a side note, given that so many of us have chronic injuries, physical limitations, or just a general proclivity towards pushing oneself to the point of injury, I'm not sure that I'd make this type of sitting a frequent practice for myself these days. This aging body doesn't need to be sitting in meditation for pain to arise; just getting out of bed in the morning does the trick.

A LASTING SENSE IMPRESSION

After meditating under Goenka's guidance for six months, my concentration and mindfulness had become very strong, and I began to have unusual experiences. I would not call these mystical, cosmic, or visionary. I believe that I was simply getting a glimpse into the biological core of my being.

At one point in my meditation retreat, when my concentration and mindfulness were perhaps as finely tuned as they have ever been, I began to notice that a distinct physical sensation appeared before each one of my thoughts. I was dumbfounded. Was I experiencing some kind of trigger in my body for thoughts, perhaps an impulse to think? When I asked Goenka about this, he just laughed and said, "Of course. Every thought is preceded by a sensation." Recent neuroscientific research reveals that, indeed, thought usually takes place rather late in the cognitive process.

Eventually I became more familiar with the pre-thought impulses I was feeling and realized that after I felt the sensation I could actually decide whether or not I wanted to become conscious of the thought. My mindfulness had begun operating beneath the thinking mind, at the very starting point of cognition, and that gave me an amazing feeling of freedom.

What was equally remarkable to me was that the pre-thought sensation arose from the middle of my chest, and not in my head. The impulse to think came from the region just below my sternum, the place that Chinese and Indian yogis have long referred to as the "heart-mind."

During this particular meditation retreat, I had another revelation that I feel somewhat reluctant to reveal because of its tinge of nihilism. Nonetheless what I understood has remained with me as a most profound glimpse into the nature of existence, and it is an experience I want to hold close at the moment of my death.

Over the course of several weeks of meditating, at times my mind would grow very silent so that only once every few minutes would a thought come knocking at the door of consciousness. Nothing ever felt as wonderful to me as that empty silence: there was not a wisp of desire or aversion for anything in the world, no impulse to move or think. At those moments of utter peace, any sensation at all, even those I would normally label as "pleasant," such as the faint sound of music or a cooling breeze, while not disturbing to me, were nothing special in the greater bliss of emptiness. I realized that sensations, even at their best, weren't actually very compelling after all. I realized that the Buddha was right when he said that sensual pleasure is a paltry thing compared to the joy that comes from peace of mind: he called that "the highest happiness."

I didn't have these experiences because I have special faculties or abilities. Anybody can have similar experiences and the insights that derive from them. It is a gift of Nature. One only needs to practice mindfulness meditation and commit to the effort of playing a little evolutionary sport.

EXERCISE
🐾 The Body Scan 🐾

In the following exercise, we will use the technique known as the "body scan" to explore basic sense impressions and our instinctual reactions to them.

The body scan is a moving mindfulness, a way to bring the quality of non-reactive investigation to all parts of the body. In this exercise we will use the scan to focus on physical sensations, and to notice the basic feelings of pleasant, unpleasant, or neutral. As we do, we may also notice the beginning of our instinctual reactions. In this exercise we are exploring the first sparks of subjective experience.

As you do this meditation, you might occasionally want to spend a few moments—perhaps lingering on some area of sensations—as you engage in a simple reflection on the life processes taking place inside you. As you feel the sensations you realize that your body is metabolizing, digesting, consuming oxygen, transporting nutrients; cells are interacting with each other, doing their own dance of life and death; microbes are feasting and moving around through your digestive system; chemicals are being secreted and absorbed; and assemblies of brain cells are firing messages, even as you reflect. What you are experiencing during the body scan exercise is the amazingly complex life of your body, taking place on its own inside you at every moment.

As you scan through the body do not look for or try to create any particular type of sensation. Simply feel whatever is naturally occurring. See if you can just experience the bare sensations, without even identifying them as "I" or "mine," or without judging them good or bad. Then be sure to take notice if some reaction does occur. If you did not consciously choose to react, then where did that reaction come from?

As you scan, you might notice sensations of tingling, itching, twitching, pressure, tension, pain, pulsation, hardness, density, heat, coolness, et cetera. But in some areas of the body you may feel nothing. This "nothing" is simply what you experience at that place in your body, and it should not be regarded as a failure. Instead, simply let your mind focus on the feeling of "nothing" for a few moments, exploring its subtler aspects. Does this nothing feel like numbness, or more like voidness or empty space? Feel the precise quality of this lack of sensation, exploring the area of nonfeeling for a little longer than other areas.

Beginning meditators should be aware that it takes some degree of concentration before we begin to feel the subtlest levels of our sensations. Nonetheless, a great deal of insight can be gained by just doing this exercise a few times.

In the following body scan we will start at the top of the head and move systematically down through the body. Once you become familiar with the act of moving your mindfulness around, however, you may want to scan your body in a different pattern. Some people scan down the body from head to toes, and then reverse the pattern and scan back up from toes to head and start over again. It is also fine to scan down the back side of the body and up the front side, or vice versa, or to scan down one half of the body lengthwise and then up the other.

Although any pattern of scanning is fine, it is important to settle on one pattern and stay with it. That helps to develop a regular and easy flow of mindful awareness, and also helps to ensure that you will not unintentionally skip over some parts of the body.

The speed of the body scan can also vary to some degree. Some meditators like to scan slowly and will devote an entire meditation session of twenty or even sixty minutes to doing one single scan. Others like to scan quickly, perhaps taking the duration of two or three breaths for one complete scan. After maturing in the practice, some meditators even scan down the body with one exhale and up with one inhale.

Beginners are advised to go more slowly. When first practicing this meditation technique, try to go very slowly for the first few scans so that you can make sure you are including all areas of your body in the scan. Even if you do speed up the scanning process, in every meditation session do at least one or two scans slowly (taking at least ten minutes) to explore all the areas of the body thoroughly.

To begin the body-scan exercise, sit or lie down in a comfortable position, close your eyes and move your attention to the very top of your head. Feel whatever sensations exist there in this moment—heat or pressure or tingling or numbness. Remember, you are not trying to create sensations, you are only feeling them.

See if you can experience the sensations without commenting on them, judging them good or bad, or claiming them as "me" or "mine." Just feel what is happening, keeping the mind as calm and still as possible. As you soften into this more neutral relationship to what you are feeling, notice any habitual reactions that do occur. Experience these unchosen movements of mind, exploring where they might be coming from and how they affect your feelings.

If you have trouble feeling any sensations or even locating the top of your head, you might imagine your in-breath flowing up to that place. During the body scan the breath can be a useful tool, helping to move your mental focus to a particular part of the body or, when it seems to get stuck someplace, helping to free it and keep it moving.

After exploring the top of the head, slowly begin to move your attention down across the forehead and over the sides and back of the head. Let your mindful awareness be as penetrating as possible, scanning through the inside of the head as well as across the surface. Can you feel your brain, its weight and density? (No judgment intended.)

Continue to move attention down the face, over the fluttery eyelids, the temples, the back of the head. Be sure to include the ears in your scan, even though you may have only a faint sense of their presence.

Move attention down over the lips and jaws, inside the mouth and down the back of the head and into the neck and throat area. Feel the sensations as you scan—solid, tingling, warmth, tension—whatever appears.

Continuing your scan, move your attention down into the shoulders and upper body. As you move through the upper torso, the chest and back, see if you can feel your insides as well as your outsides. Do you feel the solidity of the rib cage? Perhaps your insides feel like an undefined watery mass. Can you feel any movement or activity going on in there? Twitches or flowing movements. Perhaps burbling and gurgling. Just explore the torso in order to experience whatever sensations are present.

Move the awareness down through the upper arms (unless they were included in the scan of your torso), down through the elbows, into the hands and fingers. Let your mindful awareness linger for a few extra moments in the center of your palms and at the ends of your fingers. Because of their complex functioning, these areas have a lot of nerve endings and therefore usually a great deal of sensation.

Continue the scan down into the pelvic region and the lower stomach, out across the thighs, through the knee, and down the lower leg to the foot and toes. Allow your attention to remain for a few minutes at the soles of the feet and the ends of the toes. As acupuncturists point out, the soles of our feet contain nerve endings that connect to every other part of our body. Can you feel them in your sole? Your foot is very sensitive, perhaps because it once had very precise activities to perform. It still needs to sense your next step, your every step. For safety you need to feel the surface you are walking or standing on. Is it friendly or hostile?

Let your awareness sink into your feet. Feel their intelligence; feel their sensitivity. This is your base, your bottom line, your point of contact with the earth.

When you are finished with the scan, bring your attention to the top of the head again, and for a few moments just try to feel the sensations in the entire body all at once. Simply be aware of this single living organism, and all of the processes taking place that indicate life. After a few minutes of feeling the entire body, you can begin another scan.

THE SENSATIONAL EXPERIENCE

The next time you walk down a crowded city street, imagine that you are suddenly given the power to see into the workings of people's minds and nervous systems. You can actually observe the various senses picking up stimuli—light, sound, physical sensations—and flashing signals from the nerve endings into various brain centers to combine with a multitude of other signals coming from other parts of the brain and body, all of the messages coursing through the neural circuits and across the synaptic spaces, sorting, analyzing, and then sending signals back out to the muscles, ordering certain chemical releases—a shot of adrenaline here, some dopamine there—in a constant process of adjusting the physical and mental state of each person as they stroll along.

As you look you can see the signals instructing their leg muscles to move, ordering their eyes to scan for obstacles and to read the stop lights, alerting the brain centers to order the legs to pause for cars and to step around debris. And all of this is going on unconsciously, while the thinking mind is caught up in measures of success defined by something other than the ability to walk down the street.

People are split. Their bodies are walking while their minds are talking. If their imagery and thoughts were to become visible and audible to you as you pass them by, you would find most people absorbed in thinking about what they will do when they arrive at their next destination or what has occurred at the last one, or else having a good fantasy or mulling over a current or future life issue of finance, romance, or family life. You would be hearing a great babble of thinking, almost none of it having anything to do with the act of walking down the street. The thoughts may begin to sound to you like non sequiturs coming from a parade of lunatics.

Of course, this capacity of the human brain to process multiple stimuli beneath our conscious awareness is a gift of nature, quite wondrous and useful. If we had to attend consciously to a mere fraction of what confronts us in each moment, we would be overloaded, paralyzed with the demand for decisions. Nonetheless, being too far removed from where we are or from what our bodies are doing may be hazardous to our health, as well as a major source of our suffering. We become dislocated from the immediacy of our lives and the world around us.

As denizens of this civilization and evolutionary era, we have become almost totally identified with the content of our minds. This condition is both a symptom of extreme individualism and in turn feeds our sense of separateness. Most of us live—as James Joyce once remarked about one of his characters—a short distance from our bodies. In fact, we seem to live as far from our bodies as our necks are long. Heads are us!

I remember, as a college student, wondering how I could stop the endless thinking that went on in my mind, the planning for the future, the fantasizing and worrying about this or that. I felt a kinship with the existentialist philosophers, my heroes at the time, who were frustrated by their own constant cogitation and analysis, and who wished nothing more than to be in direct communion with the world. As Albert Camus wrote, "If I were a tree among trees, a cat among cats . . . this problem would not arise. This ridiculous reason is what sets me in opposition to all creation."

I believe that my years of meditation practice, often with a focus on the first two Foundations of Mindfulness—body and basic sense impressions—have brought me a new degree of intimacy with my moment-to-moment experience. I am not in some altered state of consciousness, feeling a mystical unification with the sidewalk and the bird songs, and I don't feel totally present at all times by any means. But I do believe that meditation has brought me more awareness of whatever physical activity I am engaged in, which in turn has led me to a new sense of ease and connection with my environment.

In the act of walking down the street, for instance, if I catch myself lost in thought I usually notice also that my head is leaning forward and my shoulders are somewhat tense. Furthermore, I realize that I have hardly been aware of the people passing by, the sounds, or the quality of the air. When I remember to be conscious of walking down the street, I am then able to move out of the dramas of personality in my head and to enter into contact with the world. As I walk along I can feel the air on my skin and the earth beneath me, solid and comforting. Furthermore, the people passing by become part of my life just because we are in this circumstantial moment together. When my consciousness is in my physical body or basic sense impressions, I also feel that I am not so different from everybody I pass. We all have similar walks and ways of swinging our arms; we carry the same brand of nervous system and are breathing the same air. Most of our differences are in our heads.

When we are completely identified with our thinking mind we find ourselves continually judging the world, and somewhat separated from it. Meditations on the first two Foundations of Mindfulness can bring us back into our bodies, which in turn brings us back into the environment and back into the moment. We become more aware of our biological being, our organic nature. We discover a new kind of intimacy with ourselves and our surroundings.

CHAPTER SIX

⋙ ⋘

The Third
Foundation of Mindfulness

States of Mind

Somewhere in the far past of man something strange happened in his evolutionary development. His skull has enhanced its youthful globularity; he has lost most of his body hair and what remains grows strangely. He demands, because of his immature emergence into the world, a lengthened and protected childhood. Without prolonged familial attendance he would not survive, yet in him reposes the capacity for great art, inventiveness, and his first mental tool, speech, which creates his humanity. He is without doubt the oddest and most unusual evolutionary product that his planet has yet seen.

LOREN EISELEY, *STAR THROWER*

We are temporarily identifiable wiggles in a stream that enters us in the form of light, heat, air, water, milk. . . . It goes out as gas and excrement . . . and also as semen, babies, talk, politics, war, poetry and music.

ALAN WATTS, *WHAT IS LIFE?*

A HUMAN FEELING

The Third Foundation of Mindfulness focuses attention on what Buddhist teachers often refer to as mind-states, and what we commonly call emotions. The Pali word for this foundation, *citta,* is often translated as "heart-mind," which indicates that we are looking at the feeling-tones of the mind, the different colored filters through which we perceive the world. In the Buddhist system, a mind-state can also refer to a condition of awareness, such as concentration or delusion. Generally speaking, a mind-state is what we expect a report on when we ask someone, "How are you?"

At this point on our evolutionary journey we arrive at an experience that appears to be uniquely human. What began as a simple reaction to certain sensations now becomes part of an individual drama. A response to a sound or touch is now interpreted through "you," a vast interplay of instincts, temperament, culturization, life experiences, and a complex sorting and memory system. The feelings of pleasant or unpleasant have grown more varied and nuanced, and are given names like happiness, frustration, sadness, or love. A story line has now entered the picture; a personality has appeared.

The importance of the Third Foundation of Mindfulness should be rather obvious; your mind-state is how you feel right now. And—as a correction to a popular assumption—what you *feel* is what you really get. Therefore, paying attention to your mind-states and how they are produced and altered should be very high up on your list of things to do.

As we investigate our states of mind, we should take into account the latest scientific understanding, which presents an extremely unromantic view of our most cherished human sentiments. In his book *The Emotional Brain,* neuroscientist Joseph LeDoux claims that emotions are nothing more than the feelings associated with basic survival functions. LeDoux explains that all animal species have evolved systems that handle procreation, feeding, and fight-or-flight responses. And, writes LeDoux, "when these systems function in an animal that also has the capacity for conscious awareness, then conscious emotional feelings occur." By this definition, anger or hatred are just labels we give to sensations associated with the protective instinct, while affection is simply our awareness of an evolved aspect of the procreation system. ("What's love got to do with it?")

The Buddhist sages also point out the close connection between our instinctual reactions and the resulting mind-state or emotion. In fact, this is the link between the Second and Third Foundations of Mindfulness. We react with simple approach or avoidance to a pleasant or unpleasant sensation (Second Foundation), which routinely leads to a full-blown emotional state (Third Foundation) of grasping or aversion. Like the scientists, the Buddhist sages saw that we are usually not conscious of this connection. Therefore, we take our emotions to be self-generated and freely chosen. We mistake each emotion as "I" or "self," and become completely identified and lost in it. We fail to see that emotions come with being human, that they have biological origins and important survival functions. We don't realize that they are evolution's emotions. Most important of all, the sages discovered that we do not have to be driven by these primal or habitual reactions. By bringing more consciousness to the emotional process, we can start to develop a different relationship with our feelings and behavior. We can free our hearts and minds—at least to some degree—from the chains of past conditioning, and may even learn how to cultivate the more harmonious states of mind.

> *The sage is independent. Sorrow and avarice do not cling to him as water does not stick to the lotus leaf.*
>
> THE BUDDHA, *JARA SUTRA*

The followers of the Buddha investigated the nature of their own minds with such care and precision that eventually they recognized 121 classes of consciousness and 89 different mind-states. Just as the Eskimos have many different words for snow, the Buddhist sages gave their most careful attention to that which surrounded them all the time—the colors and textures of their mind.

These explorers of the mind world presented their understanding in the *Abhidhamma,* a multi-volume primer of psychophysiology written more than two millennia ago. Buddhist scholar W. F. Jayasuriya calls this text "both a scientific treatise and a metaphysical discourse," because it not only explains how our experience is created, but also tells us how to live in harmony with those conditions. Among other things, the *Abhidhamma* gives detailed accounts of the origin and composition of mind-states, as well as the process of cognition and consciousness. In recent years, psychology and brain research alike have validated these early Buddhist models of mind, the source of which was the experiential research of thousands of people who simply observed their own minds in silent meditation.

According to the *Abhidhamma* map of mind, consciousness is the cognitive element, or *that which knows* the objects of our experience. Each moment of our knowing also passes through various psychic filters, called "mental factors." There are fifty-two of these mental factors, and they arise in different combinations to color each experience. Some are *universal* mental factors, such as sensation, perception, and attention, because they arise in every moment of consciousness. The *nonuniversal* mental factors, such as composure, restlessness, envy, and confidence, will arise as a result of instinctual urges as well as the habits of mind that each of us have acquired during the course of our life—our psychological conditioning. Some combination of the fifty-two mental factors from these two streams of karma—nature and nurture—will create the mind-state through which we view the world.

> *By your own efforts*
> *Waken yourself, watch yourself,*
> *And live joyfully.*
>   THE BUDDHA, *DHAMMAPADA*

If you check in at any given moment during the day you will notice the presence of one mind-state or another. Although this may seem obvious, the truth is that we are generally not conscious of our mind-states, their origin, or how they function in our lives. We are caught in them and by them, but we rarely notice their existence. We don't see our mind's condition, because we are *inside* that condition.

When I check to see how I am feeling, I will often discover that I am inhabited by an emotion that moved in without my permission. Sometimes I will be feeling mildly irritated or grumpy and will suddenly realize that I am hungry, and that the feeling of irritation is being generated by a low blood-sugar level. Or else I will examine a bad mood and realize that it started with some task that didn't go well in the morning or a remark someone made hours ago, but the emotional state is still operating, feeding on its own momentum. In general, I realize that I am often not exactly *conscious* of how I am feeling. And when I do check in, I discover that I am not having a feeling so much as a feeling is having me.

The instructions in the *Mahasatipatthana Sutra* tell us, quite simply, to become aware of our mind-states and emotions. "A [meditator] knows a lustful mind as lustful, a mind free from lust as free from lust; a hating mind as hating, a mind free from hate as free from hate." Since a mind-state can also be distinguished by the degree of consciousness that is present, the meditator is also instructed to notice "a distracted mind as distracted," "a concentrated mind as concentrated," "a deluded mind as deluded."

Contrary to what you might expect from a "spiritual" text, the various emotions and mind-states are neither condemned nor praised. They are first of all to be understood as natural occurrences, arising as a condition of being human—having a body, contact with the world, the feelings of pleasant, unpleasant, and neutral, and being conscious of oneself.

If we can just observe or name a mind-state, we are no longer completely identified with it; some part of us is simply aware. Once we are no longer lost in the mind-state we begin to recognize it as a function of a nature based in evolution. We see that the mind we are given has different settings—moods, speed levels, degrees of clarity—and that these change during the normal course of a day in response to various causes and conditions. As we begin to see our mind-states as somewhat impersonal, their intensity and ability to define us are diminished. Although all the different mind-states will continue to come and go, we will not be as likely to drown beneath their spells.

> *Thus any feeling whatsoever—past, future or present; internal or external; blatant or subtle, common or sublime, far or near; every feeling—is to be seen as it actually is with right understanding: "This is not mine. This is not my self. This is not what I am."*
>
> THE BUDDHA, SAMYUTTA NIKAYA

THE DISSATISFIED MIND
An Organic Blues

The First Noble Truth of Buddhism states that life is inherently unsatisfactory. There may be certain moments right after you have fulfilled one desire or another—following a meal, sex, or winning some competitive game—when you may feel satisfied for a little while. But that feeling generally doesn't last long. Often only a few minutes will pass before another desire or discomfort arises.

If you begin to check in on your mind-states, you may notice the almost constant presence of desire. Even in moments that you recognize as contentment or satisfaction, you might feel your mind moving, however slightly, into the future, or finding some little fault with the present situation.

What can truly feel embarrassing is to catch yourself desiring what you already have or desiring to be where you already are. I am sometimes aware, especially upon discovering some new beach, nature walk, or restaurant, that I will start looking forward to coming back to that place, long before I have even left it. I will be planning to return with the proper apparel, the right friends, or at a different time of day, so that I can have a more perfect experience of the place where I already am, but not really, since my mind has already moved on to my next experience of that very place.

Dissatisfaction appears to be built into the human condition, and although that may sound cruel, it is apparently in the best interest of our survival. The brain maintains a certain degree of unease running continually, keeping us monitoring the world for some advantage or danger, always a little on edge and ready for action. The motor may lie somewhere within the brain stem, perhaps in the reticular activating system or in the lateral hypothalamus. Brain research suggests that we share this perpetual unease with many forms of life and may have inherited it directly from those in the jungle or on the savannahs who needed to stay on full-time alert for both predators and prey. Eat or be eaten was the law by which they lived.

We still need to be on watch for new threats and opportunities, but the alarm system may be too sensitive for our current situation. People living in modern society who experience relative abundance and apparent security still can't seem to relax. Many live in a constant state of high alert, even though there is no lion directly at the door.

Our condition is made abundantly clear by recent psychological studies, which find that a majority of people feel most dissatisfied when they are alone with nothing special to do. (Perhaps that is why we try to keep so busy.) Being alone with nothing to do sounds like an opportunity to relax and enjoy life, but the subjects report that their minds wander and usually land on negative or anxiety-producing thoughts. It appears that our survival brain is always trying to anticipate negative situations, looking ahead, rehearsing for disasters. That is useful for a long life—if you call that living.

Planning for the future is usually motivated by some degree of fear or unease. The next time you notice yourself trying to figure out a career, family, or financial decision, also bring your attention to the feeling-tone behind that figuring. Use mindfulness to explore the emotional charge that generates the planning. Can you sense the connection between the two? Can you recognize your planning as a tool in your evolved survival kit? Nature is telling you, "Think or die!"—and you are just following orders.

The Buddha may not have known exactly where our unease and future-plan maker were located in the brain, but he understood that they are intrinsic to the human condition. He also discovered that mindfulness meditation is a way of relieving the tension. That does not mean shutting down the survival brain: psychological studies of meditators reveal that not only are they more relaxed, but they can also respond more quickly to stimuli. Meditation seems to enable people to settle more comfortably into each moment's experience and still remain alert for sudden threats and flying objects. Perhaps becoming more familiar with how our brain and nervous system operate makes them more efficient and user-friendly.

As strange as it sounds, meditation may also reveal that we are happier than we thought we were. We may discover that ancient conditioning rather than present circumstances is causing our dissatisfaction, and that this moment is quite sufficient or even wonderful, and we simply hadn't noticed.

> *Do not pursue the past. Do not lose yourself in the future.*
> *Looking deeply at life as it is in this very moment, the*
> *meditator dwells in stability and freedom.*
>
> THE BUDDHA,
> *BHADDAKARATTA SUTRA*

THE ORGANIC BLUES
Take Two

The mind-body connection has grown increasingly clear over the past few centuries, in spite of Descartes's attempt to sever the two with a thought. Neuroscience is now using computerized technologies to link various mind-states and emotions with specific areas of the brain. These discoveries are significant, not only because they have the potential to inform new treatments for mental disorders, but also because they are revealing the organic, evolutionary origins of our emotional life. Neuroscientists have taken us into the structures of our limbic system, down to where the lemur lives. They have uncovered the lair where fear, rage, passion, and lust are hiding, awaiting their respective turns in our lives.

An almond shaped structure in the brain called the amygdala (from the Greek word for almond) seems to play a central role in emotional life. Situated just above the brainstem, the amygdala was part of the primitive "nose brain," the earliest area to form in the limbic system. Neuroscientific research has shown that the amygdala tracks and controls the most basic of our feelings and reactions; it stores our emotional memories and triggers behavior based on those memories.

At first scientists believed that the amygdala had to check in with the "higher" brain centers—those associated with reason and thought—before interpreting or signaling a response to a stimulus or event. In fact, the emotional areas of the brain often do work in tandem with the rational, but recent pictures of brain activity reveal that the amygdala can also act independently, especially in a situation that is perceived as having great importance to our survival. Because of its record of success, nature has given the amygdala a privileged position of power, even over our vaunted ability to reason.

The amygdala is constantly receiving incoming signals from the environment and especially looks for trouble. If some sight or sound awakens the same sensations as a past traumatic event, the amygdala will immediately trigger an emotional reaction. For instance, when it perceives a threat, the amygdala will send signals that freeze the movement of any muscles unrelated to the emergency, and simultaneously will instruct the facial muscles to get themselves into an expression of fear or anger, all of it before *you* (or rather your thinking brain) can even blink an eye.

Although it works well in emergencies, the amygdala is not all that smart in assessing whether or not an emergency really exists. For instance, as the amygdala scans our experience for a "match"—anything that resembles a past trauma, injury, or threat—it may light on some vague approximation of a past event and react as if it were the same. Our emotional reactions could often be considered "false alarms." In other words, the emotional brain can generate mind-states—especially those of fear, anger, or passion—based on a miscalculation by the amygdala.

In his book *Emotional Intelligence,* Daniel Goleman refers to the amygdala as a "neural tripwire" that can instantaneously send signals of "crisis" to all parts of the brain and body. Goleman calls these events an "emotional hijacking" of the brain. Not only does the amygdala hijack the brain it can also hold it hostage: the adrenal and cortical stimulation caused by a strong emotional arousal can linger in our system for days. Goleman indicates that this physiological condition may be at the core of chronic worry, which he terms a "low-grade" emotional hijacking. After the amygdala is aroused to deal with one problem, even though the initial cause for arousal may be handled or dismissed, the entire system stays on maximum alert long thereafter, looking for more threats or problems upon which to fixate, feeding on itself, creating a state of continued anxiety. Perhaps the highly stressed behavior of people in modern urban society can be understood as a mass hostage-taking of our brains by alarmed amygdala.

The emotional center of the brain can also create inopportune mind-states because it takes most of its instructions from the past. The distant evolutionary past creates the hardware—the stimulus-response mechanisms and memory-storage facility—and the primary operating software is installed during our very first years of life.

In infancy and early childhood, the amygdala becomes imprinted with our first emotional memories, which we then carry with us throughout our life. One reason that these memories are so powerful is because the amygdala is one of the first parts of the brain to mature and is almost fully functional at a time when the thinking brain is just beginning to develop. Early in life the thinking brain is not yet capable of placing any nuance on emotional memories; we don't have the reasoning power to talk the amygdala down from a trauma. The shocks and seductions of the world are therefore deeply imprinted, and our memory of them becomes a preverbal, unconscious blueprint for our future emotional life.

Without knowing any details about the amygdala, the Buddha recognized its effects and the lesson to be learned. The fact is that we can each experience the results of the neural tripwires in action, or the stored emotional patterns in the amygdala being activated. The Buddha taught that what is most important to our happiness is to observe and realize for ourselves the extent to which everyday feelings are at the mercy of past conditioning. Then we can begin to gain a new perspective on our emotional life.

When I observe myself carefully in meditation, I am repeatedly amazed to watch how much my feelings get swayed and jerked around by instinctual or habitual reactions to various stimuli. Even though I have seen the process many times, I continually forget and fall into the habit of assuming that "I" am in full charge of my emotional condition. Especially during longer meditation retreats, as I watch myself through several days of activity, I will see clearly how I am automatically drawn into different mind-states. For example: I may be brushing my teeth, or walking to an interview, or sitting in meditation when suddenly a thought about my work will surface, perhaps due to a regular random recycling of work thoughts, or possibly triggered by some association with a face, a sound, or some closely related thought moving through my mind. I can almost see my survival brain (perhaps the amygdala) stamp the work thought with an "important" label, so that immediately some other part of my brain (perhaps the region known as the association cortex) will begin chewing on it, simultaneously creating some particular feeling-tone based on the overall assessment of the thought. Although I will not have made a single "conscious" choice of either thought or feeling, suddenly I will find myself anxious or elated, or lost in what meditators refer to as "planning mind."

I am continually shocked when I see this process clearly in my own mind. I realize that in "normal" life—when I am without mindfulness or any evolutionary perspective—I am completely carried away by moods that have arisen at the whim of some random sense impression or old mental habit, driven along by the engines of instinct.

Every time I see this truth again, however, I begin to feel a new sense of ease and freedom. Remembering my animal nature relieves my human nature. As I recognize the biological origin of my feelings, my usual intense identification with them begins to weaken. As a result, my mind doesn't get pushed and pulled around so much by everything that whips through my head or across my field of vision. Even though my habits and instincts are still operating, my "brain-jerk" reactions aren't quite so definitive or overwhelming. Often a moment of mindfulness will appear between a stimulus and a response, and I will be reminded that I have some new degree of choice over how I feel and behave.

I have also found that reflecting on the latest scientific knowledge of the brain can be very useful as I explore my own emotional life. Information about the functioning of the limbic system helps to explain my life experiences, and gives me a spacious, archetypal context for my feelings and even my perceptions.

INGREDIENTS FOR EMOTIONAL SOUP

We know, now, that there is a correspondence between chemical reactions in the brain and the flow of thoughts and emotions through the psyche. We know that adolescence is a chemical phenomenon, beyond the control of the victim. We know that love can be titrated in a test tube, and that avarice is inscribed in our genes. We know now that nationalism plays out its bloody scenarios across the field of GABA receptors in the brains of old men long before young ones meet to die on the battlefields. Though we don't yet know what the linkage is between chemistry and thought, there is no longer any doubt that such linkages exist, or that we are defined by them.

JON FRANKLIN, *MOLECULES OF THE MIND*

Our evolutionary karma is at least partially passed on to each of us in chemical compounds and through epigenetic expression, further signs of our elemental nature. Epigenetics is the study of changes in organisms caused by modification of gene *expression* rather than alteration of the genetic code itself.

Even stress and malnutrition are passed down over generations epigenetically and chemically. "Chemical karma" may be even more literal than we thought. In recent years neurochemists and molecular psychologists have uncovered a river of chemicals that flows along beside all of our moods and behavior. Biomolecular science is revealing a new "chemical brain" model, in which different compounds diffuse themselves throughout the system's fluids as a means of coordinating the activity of the organism. The biomolecular scientists are claiming that they have found "a second nervous system."

The very first neuroscience model of the brain and nervous system was "electrical," with brain and nerve cells communicating by "firing" signals across synaptic gaps. The chemical model does not supplant the electrical one, but rather uncovers another level of complexity. It is like seeing that an automobile's drive shaft is moved by the firing of the pistons in the engine, and then realizing that what makes the pistons move is the gasoline being ignited.

The chemical model—the second nervous system—focuses on the millions of "receptor" molecules found on the surface of each of our cells. As neuroscientist Candace Pert wrote in *Molecules of Emotion,* "If you were to assign a different color to each of the receptors that scientists have identified, the average cell surface would appear as a multicolored mosaic of at least seventy different hues—50,000 of one type of receptor, 10,000 of another, 199,000 of a third, and so forth."

The receptor molecules are the eyes and ears of our internal world, sensitive to signals from other molecules that are "diffusing" themselves throughout the fluids of our body. When the right chemical comes along, the corresponding receptor molecule wiggles and twitches into various shapes. The receptors are called "keyholes," which according to Pert are "waiting for the right chemical keys to swim up to them through the extracellular fluid and to mount them by fitting into their keyholes—a process known as binding." As Pert remarks, "It's sex on a molecular level."

Once the receptor receives the right chemical message, it sends it from the surface of the cell into the interior, which initiates a chain of biochemical events that cause the cell to create new proteins, or to secrete a particular chemical substance. Specifically, the receptors are looking for three different groups of molecules, known collectively as ligands (that which binds). The names of the ligands have become commonplace in our current world. One group are the neurotransmitters such as dopamine, serotonin, and norepinephrine, which are made to carry messages across the gaps between brain cells. A second group of ligands are the steroids: the sex hormones testosterone, progesterone, and estrogen. The third and most common of all binding chemicals are the peptides, which regulate most of our essential life processes.

The receptors and ligands are known collectively as "information molecules" because they keep all of the cells of the body in touch with each other. This biomolecular network has the ability to communicate across the neurological, endocrine, immune, and gastrointestinal systems, allowing the organism to coordinate all of its activity.

This chemically based nervous system is another part of our evolutionary inheritance. For instance, various opiate receptors and their ligands can be found in the brains of all vertebrates and even some insects. Perhaps they are a sign of nature's intrinsic mercy.

Rather than reducing our emotional life to chemicals, the second nervous system is further proof of the Buddhist principle of dependent co-arising, revealing that the entire history of life is present in every human experience. Molecules, chemicals, cells—perhaps the intelligence behind it all is "the god of small things."

GUT FEELINGS

As meditators focus on the Buddha's Third Foundation of Mindfulness, they begin to see the relationship between thinking and emotions more clearly and may be shocked to realize the extent to which feelings are leading in the dance of life. This appears to be an evolved condition. As Daniel Goleman reminds us, "There was an emotional brain before a rational brain."

As neuroscience uncovers the secrets of the brain, there is increasing evidence that our lives are guided more by "visceral" reactions than they are by reason. Most psychologists would agree, having discovered some time ago that emotions often occur beyond conscious control. Psychological research shows that even our simplest likes and dislikes can be dictated by the unconscious functions of the emotional brain.

A watershed series of experiments conducted in 1980 by social psychologist Robert Zajonc were summarized in a paper entitled "Feeling and Thinking: Preferences Need No Inferences." The studies exposed English-speaking subjects to subliminal visual patterns that were unfamiliar to them, in one case to Chinese ideograms. Later the subjects were exposed to new ideograms along with some of those already shown and asked which they preferred. Invariably, the subjects chose the previously exposed ideograms, even though they were not even aware of having seen them before. The emotional brain decided that it preferred the familiar, although the subject was not even conscious of what was familiar.

Other experiments confirm that in the very first milliseconds of perception, before the cognitive brain even recognizes an object, the emotional brain not only determines what is being perceived, but how you will feel about it. Maybe, if it was ever consulted, your thinking brain would decide it didn't like what your emotional brain likes. Which one would you believe? Which is the real *you?*

It seems that you contain multitudes, what MIT science professor Marvin Minsky calls a "society of mind," a whole group of specialists who get together to create your reality. Although the emotional brain can at times act independent of reason, most often it does not. Usually, as part of the decision-making process, the central committee of the emotional brain—itself representing many distinct agents—will consult with the central committee of the rational center.

Dr. Antonio Damasio, professor of psychology, philosophy, and neurology at the University of Southern California, finds that patients who have suffered damage to the link between the prefrontal lobes of the neocortex and the amygdala have a very hard time making decisions, or they make ones that don't lead to satisfaction or harmony in their lives. The problem seems to be that the emotional part of their brain—which knows for sure what it likes without need for justification—is not available for consultation. The rational mind, working alone, apparently gets stuck in its own reasonable balancing act and can't decide, finally, what it wants to do.

So, when reason is left out of the mix, our emotions are often inappropriate, and if emotions are left out, then reason can get caught in quibbling immobility. This could be interpreted as another sign that we are in transition—a missing link—and just starting to learn how to use our new brain regions, the latest gift of evolution. Could it be that the rational centers of the brain will increasingly replace the emotional centers? Do love and hate have a future?

I would guess that most of us, if confronted with the choice, would say that we want to hold on to our ability to experience emotions. We expect to be sentimental about our sentiments, and most of us could not imagine human life without them.

Dr. Damasio and others have found that for people whose emotional brain has been damaged, experience often seems to lose its flavor, its vitality. The emotional brain not only ensures our survival by acting as sentinel and emergency response network, but, in the process, it creates the raw material for love and hate, sadness and happiness, or what is known in Buddhism as "the ten thousand joys and sorrows." Through us the emotional brain plays out its many variations on the basic themes of push-pull, approach-avoidance—creating the full range of our distinctive human music. For now, at least, we place great value on the ability to have those feelings, perhaps because, quite simply, without them we would perish.

> *The pleasure associated with seeing beauty, including scientific "truth," may have come about during the course of evolution, just as love and biophilia—the pleasure we take in the company of other living creatures—provoke us to seek out mates and the natural environments that have been most conducive to our survival. If we did not fear death, we might be too quick to kill ourselves when troubled or inconvenienced and thus perish as a species. Belief in life's importance may not be a reflection of reality, then, but an*

evolutionarily reinforced fantasy that prejudices believers to
do what is necessary, bear whatever burdens, to survive.
LYNN MARGULIS AND DORION SAGAN, *WHAT IS LIFE?*

THE GOOD NEWS

Psychology has been telling us for years that a good deal of our thinking and behavior is motivated by unconscious brain functions, and we now have neuroscientists taking photographs of this process. Still, it is hard to accept that how we feel at this very moment was not so much of our own "choosing," but rather based on some past experience or evolutionary imperative.

Nonetheless, as we learn more about emotions we are also beginning to see how we might gain a new degree of choice and ease with them. Perhaps the latest scientific knowledge of our lack of control is what has led therapists and educators to place more emphasis on training emotional life, recognizing that it is at least as important as training the intellect.

Over the past several decades, innovative psychological methods of managing emotions similar to Buddhist insight meditation techniques have become popular in many sectors. Daniel Goleman describes programs in American school systems designed to teach emotional intelligence to children. At their core is the principle of self-awareness, or self-observation, which Goleman says "manifests itself simply as a slight stepping-back from experience, a parallel stream of consciousness that is 'meta'; hovering above or beside the main flow, awareness of what is happening rather than being immersed and lost in it." That might easily be a description of the attitude of insight meditation practice.

At the Nueva School in the San Francisco Bay Area, the social emotional learning (SEL) curriculum (originally called "Self Science") presents children with games and exercises that teach them emotional skills. They learn to recognize and name their emotions; to see the links between thoughts, feelings, and reactions; to examine whether thoughts or emotions are ruling their decisions and behavior. They are learning how to acknowledge their own temperaments and learn from them.

The Buddha would certainly approve. This program could have been taken right out of the Pali Canon, instructing meditators to investigate the origin and nature of their mind-states so that they won't become so identified with them. They will then be relieved from the suffering of primal reactivity.

> *One insight is that the thirst of craving is the basis of our suffering. The other is that by the cooling of this thirst no more suffering is produced.*
>
> THE BUDDHA, *SUTTA NIPATA*

As a simple exercise, just close your eyes and examine the feeling-tones of your mind at this moment. What is your mood? How does your mind *feel?* Because you have been reading this book, you may notice a lot of thought activity in the mind, which could feel like excitement or perhaps more like agitation. Give your current mind-state a label or name. Do you notice any other quality of mind? Do you feel satisfied, or is there some kind of desire hovering around? Perhaps a very subtle sense of anticipation or sadness exists. Where did that feeling begin? Can it be associated with any basic instinct such as survival or reproduction? Continue to examine the feeling-tone of your mind for a few minutes. Does it stay the same, or become weaker, or intensify? Do you notice different feelings appearing, perhaps flickering in and out of the edges of awareness?

Begin checking in from time to time on your mind-states. Notice their origin, frequency, and duration. Explore them with mindfulness, an attitude of nonreactive curiosity. This simple exercise can offer you an important understanding of how your inner world is created, and a soothing new perspective on yourself.

TEMPERAMENTALLY YOU

Natures and features survive to the grave.

SPANISH PROVERB

Another way to view the evolutionary origin of mind-states and emotions is to become aware of your overall disposition—what *type* of person you are. Most of us have a distinct pattern of regularly occurring mind-states, which are best expressed by the word "temperament" (from the Latin word *temperare,* meaning "to mix"). Temperament refers to any moderately stable mixture of emotional or behavioral qualities that appears in childhood due to biological factors. Temperament is who we are at birth.

Are you a worrywart? A Pollyanna? Dopey, sleepy, or grumpy?

Research led by Harvard psychology professor Jerome Kagan revealed that babies are born with a temperamental bias to be either bold or cautious individuals. Kagan found evidence that children inherit certain neurochemistries that affect how they react to novelty, causing them to be relatively inhibited or uninhibited, traits that tend to last a lifetime.

After many years of studying the origin and nature of temperament, Kagan wrote in his book *Galen's Prophecy,* "I have become more forgiving of the few friends and family members who see danger too easily, rise to anger too quickly, or sink to despair too often. I no longer blame them privately and have become more accepting and less critical of their moods and idiosyncrasies."

Throughout history we have recognized that people come in just a few basic types. The ancient Greeks believed that a mixture of the four humors of yellow bile, black bile, blood, and phlegm combine to produce a person's inner state or temperament. The four humors were also associated with the elements of earth, air, fire, and water, and the qualities they produced were described as either cold or dry, warm or moist. You appeared in this life with a certain temperature and texture, with a basic "feel" to you.

The second-century physician Galen defined an ideal personality as one that contained a balance of the four humors. A preponderance of one humor could make a person melancholic, sanguine, choleric, or phlegmatic—a less ideal type. A melancholy person, for instance, was characterized by Galen as cool and dry due to an excess of black bile, while an excess of blood created a warm, moist, sanguine personality.

Ancient Chinese medicinal systems also posited that temperament was created by a mixture—not of substances such as bile or phlegm, but of energies. The primary two energies in Chinese Taoist typology are the regenerative, receptive, earthbound force of *yin* and the active, creative cosmic force of *yang*. Although people inherit a certain mixture of these two that stays relatively stable through life, the balance changes all the time. Like the ancient Greek system, traditional Chinese methodology associated a person's temperamental qualities with the elements of earth, air, fire, and water, and also included the tempers of metal and wood in the mix

What temper might you be? You could check by noticing how much you bend, or how "straight" you are in your approach to life. Does your soft or hard side show? Although we are all made of flesh and bones, we have different ways of holding them.

Another typology, originating in the Islamic Sufi tradition and currently popular in modern psychology, is the enneagram system, which places people into one of nine essential types. Most popular of all typologies, however, is astrology, which says that your faults, dear Brutus, as well as your finer attributes, lie somehow in your stars. According to astrology, your most predominant mind-states are coordinated with the configurations of the heavens at the time of your birth and at each subsequent moment of your life.

Contemporary science generally dismisses these systems of human typing as either conjecture or mere hogwash, and meanwhile has come up with its own determinants of temperament. Evolutionary biology has now replaced the humors, yin-yang energies, stars, and enneagram numbers with various twists in the thread of molecular DNA. Someday, perhaps, instead of tea leaves or astrological signs, we will go to a lab to get our genes read. At some future time, this scientific belief may be given no more credence than most people now give to the humors, but for the time being, elementary nature has been broken down into elementary particles.

LOOSE GENES

After years of sitting on my meditation cushion, I had become some-what familiar with my particular package of mind-states, but I was nonetheless somewhat startled to read about a breakthrough in genetic science that pointed to the possible culprit behind my personality.

A lengthy study by the National Institutes of Health (NIH), issued in January 1995, reported on the discovery of a variation of a certain gene that seems to select for a common personality trait called "novelty-seeking behavior." I immediately suspected they were talking about me. The geneticists seemed to be telling me that my tendency to seek new experiences was actually implanted inside me by my genes. This could explain why my parents' warnings about engaging in adven-turous behavior often went unheeded.

The NIH study was quite graphic in describing the shape of my excitable genes. It turns out that novelty-seekers have an extra-long dopamine receptor on certain genes, and dopamine is the chemical neurotransmitter most closely linked to pleasure and sensation seeking. An extra-long receptor would possibly attract more dopamine into the system and thereby influence novelty seeking. (Freud might have had something else to say about having an extra-long receptor.)

Many scientists believe that 50 percent of all novelty-seeking behav-ior is genetically based, and furthermore that genes account for perhaps

10 percent of the actual difference in novelty-seeking behavior between one person and the next. In other words, most of us are programmed by nature to be somewhat curious, but some, perhaps myself included, are destined to be extra curious. Although in meditation I had seen a persistent pattern of mind-states arising independent of my will, I still believed that I was creating my basic attitude toward life. Instead of the dog wagging the tail, however, it may be that the tail of the dopamine receptor is wagging the dog.

Previous research had found genes that select for many behavioral illnesses, including schizophrenia and alcoholism. The discovery of the novelty-seeking gene, however, marks the first time that a typical personality trait has been typed.

Dr. C. Robert Cloninger, of the Washington University School of Medicine, says that evidence for the genetic connection to personality is growing stronger; he is convinced that scientists will find genes that select for one of four "basic building blocks of normal temperament": novelty seeking, avoidance of harm, reward dependence, and persistence. No doubt you are in there somewhere, dear reader. There is growing evidence that your most persistent mind-states—no matter how twisted—may be an expression of the twists in your threads of DNA. Our personalities appear to have their roots in very primal energies—fear, curiosity, desire—with each of us getting a particular mix at birth.

If the Buddha were alive today he could say "I told you so," although he probably wouldn't. Throughout his teaching he counsels his followers to examine what exactly constitutes this thing they call "self" or personality. He says they should ask themselves: "This construction (self)—what is its cause, its arising, its ancestry, its origin?" Even though he wasn't likely to have known about genes, the Buddha understood clearly that we are not the creator of our personality. He realized that the past was somehow operating through every aspect of our being.

The Buddha taught that personality is constructed out of five different components—body, feelings, perception, mental life, and consciousness. Upon examination we can see that none of these are self-created: each component appears at birth as part of the human condition.

The Buddha also taught that all of us are born with a powerful instinct or underlying tendency toward belief in "the conceits of 'I' or 'mine.'" We therefore regard every experience as happening to a distinct person who, it turns out, we have falsely constructed out of nonpersonal elements.

According to the Buddha's teaching, if we can see the impersonality of the processes that we call self, our suffering will be greatly diminished. We will no longer cling so desperately to our image of ourselves or our various experiences. As the Buddha counseled his followers: "Whatever there be of form, of feeling, perception, mental formations, or consciousness . . . one should understand according to reality and true wisdom: 'This does not belong to me; this am I not; this is not my Self.'"

I believe that the Buddha would have embraced the discoveries of evolutionary biologists and possibly used their findings as aids in his teaching. Like these scientists, the Buddha took things apart to see how they are constructed, exploring the causes and conditions that produced the human condition. He could have pointed to the influence of genes, chemical compounds, and brain structures on our every thought and feeling. He might have used this knowledge as evidence that when it comes to those thoughts and feelings, in fact, "This does not belong to me; this am I not; this is not my Self."

> *A king hears the sound of a lute and is enchanted, so he asks his servants to bring him that sound. The servants bring the lute, and have to explain to the king that the sound does not exist independently, but is created out of the separate elements of strings, box, and bow. Just as the king could not find the sound of the lute, so we cannot find the self.*
>
> THE BUDDHA, *SAMYUTTA NIKAYA*

TYPES OF BUDDHISTS

Different schools of Buddhism have named their own personality types. The Tibetan Tantric Buddhists describe five different "Buddha families" into which each one of us is temperamentally born. Each Buddha family embodies a general style or stance toward the world, and members of each family have both enlightened and neurotic possibilities. For instance, the *vajra* (diamond) family has the quality or "feel" of sharpness and strength. In its enlightened form, this diamond energy might manifest as penetrating insight into the nature of things, a discriminating wisdom. The neurotic aspect of the diamond family would be a sharpness of manner, anger or prejudice, cutting or demeaning of others. In the tantric tradition, the Buddha families are archetypes, helping us to recognize and honor our basic nature while at the same time showing us how to transform the neurotic aspects of that nature into more awakened and satisfying qualities.

The Buddhist Elders' tradition divides human beings into just three temperamental types based on whether our stance toward the world is one of greed, aversion, or delusion. Although this delineation may sound simplistic, if you begin to examine your own mind-states, you will see how—in spite of many nuances—they can all fall into one of these categories. Furthermore, if we are honest with ourselves, most of us will notice a certain predominance of either greed (desire, eagerness, planning, hoping), aversion (distaste, irritation, hatred, distrust), or delusion (confusion, indecision, being unclear on the concepts and/or the instructions).

The *Visuddhimagga,* a commentarial text from the Elders' tradition, describes the characteristic behavior of each of the three types in everyday situations, such as walking, talking, and even getting ready for bed. "When they sit or they lie down to go to sleep . . . one of deluded temperament spreads their bed all awry and sleeps mostly face downward with their bodies sprawling. When woken, they get up slowly, saying

'Huh?' One of angry temperament walks as though they were digging with the points of their feet, puts their foot down quickly, lifts it up quickly. When one of greedy temperament sees even a slightly pleasing visible object, they look long as if surprised. They seize on trivial virtues, discount genuine faults, and when departing, they do so with regret as if unwilling to leave."

After becoming more familiar with my own mind-states, I find that I am a greed type. That does not mean, of course, that I am never deluded. The label only refers to my most basic attitude, my most frequent mind-states. Nor is the label meant as a putdown. Its purpose is simply to show me the particular temperament I was given by fate, the instrument I was assigned to learn on in this life.

Each of us plays our variation on some broad temperamental theme. So that while my greedy mind-states usually involve getting some kind of experiential treat, other greed types may be more interested in material possessions. And I would guess that many people involved in Buddhist practice who consider themselves greed types would have to admit, along with me, that they often experience a mind-state that is filled with desire for a mind-state that is free of desire.

> *Which is your true self, the self of yesterday, that of today, or that of tomorrow for whose preservation you clamor?*
>
> THE BUDDHA

Whether we are greed or delusion types, sanguine or melancholy, Sagittarius or Libra, many of us still believe that we can somehow change our temperament. On one side, we have evolutionary biology showing us the powerful influence of brain structure and chemicals on our personality, while on the other side, psychology tells us how thoroughly we are shaped by our early childhood years. Yet, strangely enough, while the main debate in science is over the relative powers of nature and nurture, the prevailing belief in our culture continues to be that we create ourselves. People even seem to think they can get a temperament transplant. Much of the New Age movement that emerged in the 1970s was based on the premise that you can trade in the old you and get yourself a new you, perhaps someone you can live with more easily. The evidence of psychologists, genetic scientists, and meditators alike would indicate otherwise.

The idea that our personalities are somewhat hardwired is certainly not news to meditators. People who have been engaged in contemplative practices for any length of time would have to admit, often to our chagrin, that our personalities do not change all that much. In meditation we watch certain patterns of mind-states repeat over and over, often with maddening regularity.

What the meditator can also learn, however, is how to become familiar with those recurring patterns without getting lost or too identified with them. As the spiritual teacher Ram Dass liked to admit, "I haven't gotten rid of a single one of my neuroses. But they don't have the power to define me anymore."

Mindfulness allows us to see that these persistent mind-states are not self-created and that acknowledgment changes our relationship to them. We realize that our basic timidity or aggressiveness comes from some other life, or some other phase of life. When we see the ancient sources of our personality, its demands and drama no longer cast such a powerful spell over us. After a few years of meditation practice, we can even learn how to occasionally ignore ourselves. And what a relief that can be.

One suggestion is to regard your personality as a pet. It follows you around anyway, so give it a name and make friends with it. Keep it on a leash when you need to, and let it run free when you feel that is appropriate. Train it as well as you can, and then accept its behavior, but always remember that your pet is not you. Your pet has its own life, and just happens to be in an intimate relationship with you, whoever *you* may be, hiding there behind your personality.

*What I want most is to spring out of this personality, then to
sit apart from that leaping.*

I've lived too long where I can be reached.

RUMI, UNSEEN RAIN

THERAPY FOR EVERYBODY

*There is only one core issue for all psychology. Where is the
"me?" Where does the "me" begin? Where does the "me"
stop?*

JAMES HILLMAN, ECOPSYCHOLOGY

As we examine our mind-states through the Buddha's Third Foundation
of Mindfulness, we are entering into the territory of Western psychology, which has also been inquiring into the question "Who am I?" In
these psychotherapeutic modalities, however, the focus is generally on
personal biography, the circumstances of an individual life. This emphasis was, of course, shaped by the cultural attitudes that this psychology
was born to serve.

Some psychologists lyrically describe their therapy as a way to turn
ghosts into ancestors, a way to show us who from our past is spooking
us, and how to then accept them as part of our family. During a period
of psychotherapy in the 1970s, I was given a personal glimpse into this
process. The therapeutic relief came when I finally began to hear the
harsh self-critic that lived in my head as the voice of one of my parents.
Once I recognized that the voice was not my own, I no longer had to
believe in it so completely: it no longer could define me.

For one thing, I realized that the critical voice had been directed at
a boy of three or nine or fifteen, yet I (my amygdala?) was carrying it
through my life. As I got some distance from the voice of my parent, I
also began to hear the pain and confusion in it, and as a result I started

to feel compassion for the person speaking. I finally began to accept the parental ghost as an ancestor.

Finding one of my parents inside my head is something that doesn't surprise me now, but it did at the time. In retrospect, I regard that discovery as the first crack in my solid, separate sense of self. After recognizing that one of the voices inside my head was not me, I naturally started to wonder about the identity of the others. Was my psyche full of alien invaders? Perhaps, as Norman O. Brown wrote in *Love's Body,* "A person is never himself but always a mask; a person never owns his own person, but always represents another, by whom he is possessed. And the other that one is, is always ancestors." According to most evidence, it would seem that during childhood we ingest our parents and then spend the rest of our lives trying to digest them. The science of epigenetics shows us that we can inherit dispositions directly from our parents and grandparents.

Mindfulness meditation can be a powerful aid in psychotherapy. It is one thing to recognize the ingested voices or old patterns of mind that foster our misery, and quite another to soften them. In meditation we get the chance to observe the old conditioning over and over again, without reacting in the usual way, and thereby can begin to free ourselves from its hold. The process is akin to going to therapy for years and years, going over the same material until it loses its charge.

Sigmund Freud himself suggested that psychotherapists attend to their clients with "evenly suspended attention," which is actually a fine description of mindfulness. Ideally, the psychotherapist takes the attitude of the neutral observer who doesn't react to the story you are telling from the couch, but just nods and occasionally says, "Uh huh. Uh huh. And what else?" That is precisely the voice of an investigating mindfulness, sitting inside us in meditation as a calm and accepting witness to whatever arises in our psyche. Occasionally the good doctor inside us nods and says, "Uh huh. And what else?" And they never even send us a bill.

In mindfulness meditation, people learn how to observe for themselves; they begin to let the patterns of personality appear without either repressing them or getting lost in their content. Carl Jung suggested a similar process as essential to self-awareness and healing. He wrote, "We must be able to let things happen in the psyche. For us, this is an art of which most people know nothing. Consciousness is forever interfering, helping, correcting, and negating, never leaving the psychic processes to grow in peace." The *nonreactive, non-interfering* attitude of mindfulness seems to be just what the doctor ordered.

> *Eventually you will see that the real cause of the problem is not life itself. It's the commotion the mind makes about life that really causes the problems.*
>
> MICHAEL A. SINGER, THE UNTETHERED SOUL

As we simply observe ourselves in meditation, a deeply therapeutic process naturally occurs. Essentially, the ego becomes exposed to its own impossible dreams: it begins to notice the futility of its unending struggles. In meditation, the egoic self realizes that it will never "get it together," at least not enough so that it stays together.

This insight also reveals an alternative to the satisfaction that we seek by trying to rearrange the world to our liking—a satisfaction that comes from simply relaxing into the present moment's experience. Slowly but surely, meditation teaches the ego that when it does relax, we do not immediately disintegrate into madness and the world does not fall apart. The meditator becomes more comfortable with the imperfect and insubstantial conditions of life, and thereby finds a new kind of fulfillment.

We are not transcending the ego in meditation, but rather developing and using the ego to see through itself. This is the view of psychotherapist Mark Epstein, offered in his book *Thoughts without a Thinker,* which describes the unique psychological contributions offered by the teachings of Buddhism. It is certainly encouraging to think that our egoic self could become confident enough to relax occasionally, or even to acknowledge its own transient, illusory nature. And when the ego no longer takes itself too personally or too seriously, that is what is known as "self-liberation."

Although psychologists have focused on the individual biography as the source of our suffering, most would also agree with the Buddha about the universal nature of human neurosis and dissatisfaction. Psychoanalyst Otto Rank believed that at the root of our common suffering lies our "fear of life," or what Mark Epstein calls "original separation anxiety." We fear our life because it seems to pull us out of primal union with all things. Meanwhile, we also fear our death, since we can't know where it will take us. Rank writes, "Between these two fear possibilities, these poles of fear, the individual is thrown back and forth all his life, which accounts for the fact that we have not been able to trace fear back to a single root, or to overcome it therapeutically."

Rank may not have been aware that he was echoing the Buddha's Second Noble Truth, which says that basically our lives are poised between the two primal urges to exist and not to exist. The Buddha had also seen this tension as the baseline of our common nervous disorders.

Freud himself recognized that we all exhibit symptoms of the psychological disease known as the human condition. He said that while his therapy could perhaps relieve someone's psychotic misery, it would only be in exchange for "everyday human unhappiness."

Freud came to believe that we could never truly reconcile the ego to the impossibility of finding lasting security or fulfillment, let alone everlasting life. The egoic self—that someone who we believe is managing our life—would forever remain in denial, struggling in vain to solidify and satisfy itself. Freud seems to have concluded that these generic aspects of our suffering are beyond the scope of the therapist.

Meanwhile, in direct contrast, the Buddha directs his therapy— mindfulness meditation—to these very core issues of human existence.

He discovered a way to relieve his own "ordinary human unhappiness," and spent the rest of his life teaching the method to others.

Mark Epstein calls the Buddha "the original psychoanalyst." Rather than have his followers lie down on a couch, however, the Buddha had them sit upright on a pillow. He also did not then listen to their life history or ask them to talk of their individual emotional issues. Instead, he gave them a method for observing themselves, and told them to focus on the universal processes and natural laws that create all human suffering. Rather than focus on their individual conditioning, he told them to examine their human condition.

While psychotherapy can show us how our personality is shaped by the events of our individual biography, Buddhist meditation reveals the even stronger influence of life's biography. In meditation we learn that our joys and sorrows depend as much on the structure of our nervous system as they do on how we were toilet-trained. We come to the understanding that our biography doesn't begin on our birthday, but long before, way back at the beginning of life.

Meditation allows a process of deconditioning to take place, perhaps even at the instinctual level. By applying mindfulness, a meditator seems to be able to soften automatic reactions to stimuli—or at least catch those reactions quickly—thus weakening the primal compulsions and relieving the suffering that might otherwise have been generated by them.

Buddhist meditation is not a substitute for the methods of contemporary psychology, but rather a companion. It is a *psycho-spiritual* practice. It reveals to us what it means to be human, and how to both acknowledge and enhance our life as sentient beings. The fact is that we have ghosts living inside us that are much older than even our great-great-grandparents. These are the ghosts of our biological past—the Earth, the chemicals, the cellular life, the animals—and perhaps by getting to know them in meditation we can also turn them into ancestors. When we touch and honor all of them, we might find our place in the world. We can rejoin the family of life.

RAPTURE HAPPENS!

A major goal of spiritual practice is to clear our mental space of the intellectual and emotional garbage we have been collecting . . . and to provide space for the experience of true relaxation and enjoyment.

TULKU THONDUP, *THE HEALING POWER OF MIND*

While Buddhist psychology considers all humans to be somewhat neurotic, Buddhist therapy teaches us how to manage and even transform our ordinary human mind-states. Sometimes this process is referred to as "cultivation" of mind, a word that evokes the image of tending a garden so that it produces what you want to grow rather than weeds. In some traditions, the process is called "purification" of mind, or even "training" of mind, but all the labels point to the possibility of change, and to our ability—itself a gift from evolution—to generate more feelings of contentment or compassion.

The Buddha considered a peaceful mind—one that is not pulling toward any desire or away from any annoyance—to be in the state of highest happiness. This condition is a long, long way from what the evolutionary scientists might consider possible, but then, so was the discovery of subatomic reality without a bubble chamber. Furthermore, when the Buddha said that peace was the highest happiness he was not pointing to some impossible, idealistic goal, but to an entirely new way of understanding happiness and satisfaction. He was saying that it does not exist somewhere outside yourself.

Sometimes the practice of meditation makes this truth perfectly clear by moving us into supramundane, transcendent states of mind. During my first years of meditation, for instance, I would occasionally slip into a state of great serenity. Thoughts and physical sensations would fade into the background, and I would experience an all-encompassing peace. At other times, a shivering kind of pleasure would begin coursing through my body, and I would end up shaking with waves of energy. These states came about spontaneously, until I was taught how to enter them intentionally during meditation.

After many years of Buddhist practice, I began to study and experiment with these states, known as "mental absorptions" (*dhyanas*), which usually can be entered into only when one's concentration is very strong. These mind-states are well-documented "rest and recreation" stops on the path of Buddhist meditation and can offer a new understanding of happiness or joy.

The shivering-pleasure state is known by the name "rapture" (*piti*). After entering this state several times, I began to feel it as a kind of energized satisfaction. The *Visuddhimagga* compares rapture to other kinds of happiness: "Minor happiness is only able to raise the hairs on the body. Momentary happiness is like flashes of lightning at different moments. Showering happiness breaks over the body again and again like waves on the seashore. Uplifting happiness can be powerful enough to levitate the body and make it spring up into the air. . . . But when pervading (rapturous) happiness arises, the whole body is completely pervaded, like a filled bladder, like a rock cavern invaded by a huge inundation."

Just as the relaxed states of mind available in ordinary meditation have changed my definition of satisfaction, some of these supramundane states have changed my definition of pleasure. After experiencing rapture one can also move into states of "joy," "equanimity," and "infinite space," to name a few, and while it might sound strange or surprising, these states are available to almost anyone who undertakes the training.

As we explore the intensity of mind-states in meditation, it's unfortunately not just the fun ones. We also explore the intensity of our pain. In the *Visuddhimagga,* the sages describe the feeling of hatred or ill-will (*dosa*), for instance, as it appears in the clarity of mindfulness: "It has the characteristic of savageness, like a provoked snake. Its function is to spread, like a drop of poison, or its function is to turn up its own support, like a forest fire. It should be regarded as like stale urine mixed with poison."

This is what hatred feels like. And this is what hatred does, not to the object being hated, but rather to the one who hates: it poisons and burns up its own support. Here's the law of karma, making us miserable here and now.

Strange as it sounds, we often do not really *feel* how our mind-states make us feel. In both the Tibetan and Buddhist Elders' traditions, there are exercises designed to teach meditators how to sustain difficult mind-states—without getting lost in them—so that they can be deeply felt and explored. In a practice known as *Chod,* for instance, Tibetan tantric Buddhists engage the imagination as a way to enter fully into a difficult feeling. First the meditator is told to visualize his or her fear, anger, sorrow, or greed as a demon, and then to invite that demon to come and feast on the meditator's energy or "essence." The visualized demons are often based on fierce-looking Tibetan deities with half-animal, half-human faces, hair wild or in flames, bulging eyes, long fangs dripping blood. The meditators are instructed to kindly urge this visualized demon/emotion to consume their very being. As one teacher of Tibetan Buddhism, Tsultrim Allione, told me in a conversation, "We usually don't feed our demons well enough because we don't like those parts of ourselves. In Chod practice, however, in contrast to killing the dragon, the usual procedure in the hero's journey, we nurture the demon until the dualistic battle between ourselves and the demon disappears."

What the Tibetan Buddhist sages realized is that when we resist difficult emotions they get held in place, but when we acknowledge them (without either acting them out or repressing them) they begin to lose their power. Once they are seen as archetypal characters, the mind-states lose their intense personal quality. "My fear" comes to be seen as "our fear," or animal fear, inherited from life and all its previous struggles.

Similarly, teachers in the Path of the Elders often encourage meditators to exaggerate their feelings. If I am feeling bored or restless in meditation, for instance—which happens quite frequently—I will try to give myself over completely to the restlessness until my mind and body begin to feel like an exploded bomb that cannot escape its casing, with every single molecule desperately seeking release. Of course, I could just get up from meditation and find some way to amuse or distract myself. But if I sit with (on) this bomb of restlessness, I learn that I have the capacity to experience difficult feelings without reacting in the habitual ways. Some kind of freedom emerges from the struggle. As I let the restlessness grow monstrous, it also begins to take on its own life. It is no longer "me" or "mine," but primal agitation living through me. It becomes a testament to the fact that I am alive.

In many Buddhist schools, meditators are trained to arouse certain "wholesome" mind-states of loving-kindness or compassion. These methods of *practicing* a feeling sounded very strange to me at first. Somehow, I had come to believe that feelings should be spontaneous, and that trying to evoke them would be artificial or false. I think my response arose from the fact that, for the most part, the culture I grew up in did not provide education or training in emotional life, except perhaps in repressing it. I simply did not imagine that feelings could be learned or strengthened.

Most schools of Buddhism have methods for doing just that. The tools or "skillful means" almost always involve mindfulness, often with the help of imagination and visualization, and usually include a regular practice of meditation. With continuing practice, meditators typically learn to move in and out of feelings without being as driven by them and can practice cultivating states of peace and loving kindness.

Out of the 121 classes of consciousness which are discussed in
Buddhist psychology, sixty-three are accompanied by joy and

only three are painful, while the remaining fifty-five classes are indifferent. A stronger refutation of pessimism than this is hardly possible. How deluded is man, that he mainly dwells in those three painful states of consciousness, though there are overwhelmingly more possibilities of happiness.

LAMA GOVINDA, *THE PSYCHOLOGICAL ATTITUDE OF EARLY BUDDHIST PHILOSOPHY*

EXERCISES

The following exercises are some simple ways to begin learning about the nature and function of your own mind-states. You may remember a song lyric that went, "I just dropped in to see what condition my condition was in." That is excellent advice for becoming more conscious of mind-states or emotions.

❧ Minding Your Mind ❧

You can begin with a very simple determination to pay attention to your shifting moods. Over the course of a few days or a few weeks, decide that you will check in two or three times a day to see what is going on inside of you. Just ask yourself, "How are you?" "What are you feeling?" "Which colored glasses are you wearing at this moment?"

This instruction may sound somewhat strange, as you think, "I always know what is going on in my mind: it is *me!*" But when you begin to drop in with mindfulness, you may be startled at the new perspective you will gain.

As you begin checking in, try to maintain an attitude of curiosity and acceptance. Just notice what is taking place. As the Buddha says: "A [meditator] knows a lustful mind as lustful, a mind free from lust as free from lust; a hating mind as hating, a mind free from hate as free from hate . . . a distracted mind as distracted."

As you pay closer attention to your emotions, begin to explore their origins as well. Examine what triggers them. What sets you off? Notice if there was a chain reaction of mood that led to this moment's feeling.

As you check in, notice if certain feelings have a schedule for occupying your mind. What is the general mood or attitude every morning at seven o'clock? At noon? At dusk? Are these mental attitudes related to any bodily functions? If these moods arrive at regular times or intervals, who is doing the scheduling?

❧ *The Sensations of Emotion* ☙

Mind-states are often so subtly seductive or so primally demanding that we get completely identified and carried away by them. If we want to explore emotions we need to develop methods of holding on to them without getting sucked into their vortexes. One way to accomplish this is to focus on the actual physical sensations of our emotions, the feelings that occur in the body and that are associated with a particular mind-state.

Staying with physical sensations helps to extract us somewhat from the personal stories that surround an emotion; we are then able to hold the feeling with a more curious and independent attention.

When you notice a mood or emotion, bring your mindfulness to the sensations you are feeling in the body. Where is the physical location of your emotion? Does it reside in the head, neck, or shoulders? Is your fear or anxiety felt only in your stomach, or also in your legs? Where in your body do you feel happiness?

What does the emotion *feel* like? Is it tense, heavy, soft, hard, hot, cold, tingling, buoyant? Is it solid or liquid or gaseous?

After you have located and begun feeling the physical sensations of an emotion, remain with those feelings for a while, holding them with a tender mindfulness. Notice what happens to the sensations, if they move, or change. Fully experience and explore the physical nature of your current mind-state.

🍂 *Name That Tune* 🍂

When you first notice a particular mood or mind-state, you may also want to give it a simple name, such as "anxiety," "elation," "restlessness." Indigenous peoples believed that by naming a force or an animal you gained strength in your relationship with it; naming something is proof that it has been seen.

Labeling a mind-state also helps to create a separation between the observing self and the associated feeling. We gain some independence, however slight, so that we can investigate further. You might object that you don't want to distance yourself from your feelings, but the process of disidentification will actually allow you to come closer to them. When they aren't so overwhelming or defining, you will be capable of having a more intimate and conscious experience of all your emotions.

Naming or labeling also begins to lend an archetypal or universal quality to your emotional life. Naming your feelings as you are feeling them gives them a life of their own.

🍂 *The Color of Anxiety* 🍂

In order to better experience and explore emotions, you can also give them shapes, textures, and colors. Bring them alive, making them vivid presences inside you. For example, if you feel sadness, let yourself visualize it as the proverbial dark cloud.

Anxiety may take on a certain shape or color for you. To me it suggests a thin gray line of visible vibrating static, such as you might see on a screen or video monitor. Ill will or hatred is often seen as red or orange, and its shape is that of fire, and its sound is a roar.

Just as the ancients did, give your emotions characteristics of the elements of nature. That is, after all, what they are. Let emotions be storms, with or without lightning. Let the repetitive waves of jealousy or fear be like the ocean's waves, crashing over your beachhead.

❦ All the World's a Stage ❦

You can also give your mind-states characters to play. As Walt Whitman pointed out, we contain multitudes, so bring them to life. A scoundrel may be currently ruling your mind, sneering at the world. Perhaps a hunter is currently housed in your heart-mind, focused and cunning, looking for an advantage with certain people or goals in your life.

We have all sorts of emotional characters inside us, so why not let them interact with each other. For instance, Vietnamese Zen master Thich Nhat Hanh reminds us that we may harbor an angry, frustrated child, as well as a kind and nurturing mother. So, if the angry child gets aroused, we could just evoke the loving mother inside of us to take care of it. Thich Nhat Hanh says, "Think of holding anger like a mother holding a baby."

We are a jumble of characters: heroes and scoundrels, clowns and scholars, lovers and murderers, and yet when they each appear we forget about the others. We take our current mind-state to be who we are.

At meditation classes, I often tell people to imagine exchanging their mind with the person sitting next to them. Even though the details and names would be changed, the plot lines would likely be very similar, and the chief characters would have similar conflicts and motivations. We are not that different—all of us just looking for security and love in this particular culture and phase of evolution. Of course, it would be easier to be the mindful observer of someone else's life. One would not become so identified with the heroes and villains.

Animals also make good representatives for our emotions and can provide a sense of the evolutionary origin of our feelings. For instance, when you check in you may notice that your mind-state is like a scared rabbit or mouse, nervously twitching and sniffing for the danger you know will arrive at any moment. Or maybe you are going around with your teeth bared, like a mad dog.

And what is the sound of your current mind-state? Growling, snarling, purring, tweeting? I can sometimes hear my ill will as a laughing hyena, while my longing usually sounds like a howling coyote.

Make up an entire mythology out of your own personality—people, animals, elements of nature—or just an inner paint box full of colors and shapes, and each time the shape or character appears in your life simply acknowledge and experience it with as much curiosity and independence as possible. As long as we remember that no single emotion defines us, we can gain enough presence of mind to bring playfulness and imagination to our emotional life, along with mindfulness, of course.

❧ Feelings . . . Oh, Oh, Oh, Oh . . . Feelings ❧

As part of a good evolutionary education, begin to notice how many of your emotional states can be associated with particular instinctual or primal urges. For instance:

Sexual drive. Are you in heat a good part of the day? How much does a fixation on the possibility of a new sexual encounter determine your mind-state? What is the actual feeling of that continual desire? Is the anxiety about your appearance or your performance at work somehow related to sexual goals? Notice how the urge to keep your genetic information alive manifests itself in your life, wearing one disguise or another.

Anxiety or fear. Is anxiety your most common mind state? If it is, can you sense how much of this anxiety—planning, hoping, rehearsing the future—is related to the survival instinct? In modern culture, remember, your survival probably involves the maintenance and success of your personality, status, likability, and so on. Can you sense that your anxiety about earning money or even finding pleasure may have some connection to the basic fear of extinction? Creating a larger context and story for your feelings may help ease their intensity.

Jealousy or envy. How often during the day do you wish you were having the experiences, possessions, or life of someone else? Our culture fosters this mind-state at every turn. Notice how you feel when you see certain advertisements or pictures of happy, fulfilled people. Can you sense any connection between your feelings of envy or competition and a basic survival instinct?

Self-judging, self-critical feelings. A popular and useful meditation exercise for modern life is to take one period of meditation, or a single day of checking in, and count how many times our emotional state is one of displeasure with ourselves. Where did we get these critical, disparaging voices in our heads? We certainly don't choose to have them around. How often during the day are you judging yourself? In comparison to someone else? In comparison to some image you have for yourself or that someone else had for you?

Desire. According to the Buddha, desire and aversion (the desire to avoid something) are what rule our lives. Pay close attention and notice how often you find some desire or dissatisfaction present in your mind. Recognize it as the hum of the hypothalamus, the rhythm track of the survival brain, as sure and steady as the beat of your heart. As you check in, also let yourself feel that constant, insidious pushing and pulling of your mind, the primal nervous disorder refusing to let you rest in this moment's experience. Honor the desire and dissatisfaction for its evolutionary success; curse it for denying you fulfillment or satisfaction. And remember, you don't have to take it so personally.

❦ Priming the Primal Pump ❦

Not only can we practice observing our ordinary, daily mind-states, but we can also use memory or imagination to evoke certain feelings, just for the sake of demystifying them. We can practice becoming familiar and comfortable with even our most difficult emotions.

Remembering or imagining certain scenes or events can arouse the most primal of feelings. The classical meditations on one's own death, for instance, can bring with them strong fear, self-judgment, or guilt. Just imagining a recent insult or problem can bring back the feeling that accompanied it.

Take one or two meditation sessions and just let yourself recall or imagine a scene that will provoke your fear, jealousy, anger, greed, or despair. You know what scene or image will work for you. If you can't seem to arouse the feeling, try again another time. Or try a different scene or· a different feeling.

If you do evoke the feeling, let yourself feel it. Locate it in the body, name it, let it come alive. Let it become as big as it wants. Exaggerate it. Exercise your ability to experience strong emotions without being defined or overwhelmed by them.

As you end any of these meditation experiences—especially those that involve intense imagery or emotion—be sure to bring your awareness back to the breath before opening your eyes or standing up, letting yourself rest in the comfort of this pulse for a few minutes at least, and even arousing some compassion for yourself. Let yourself return slowly into the life and conditions of the present moment.

❧ Mind over Mind: Transforming Emotions ❧

The breath is commonly used in Buddhist meditation as an aid in transforming emotions. Often it is employed by meditators in connection with imagination or visualization to foster some new feeling-tone of mind. In the *Sutra on the Full Awareness of Breathing (Anapanasati Sutra)*, the Buddha instructs his followers to infuse breath with soothing or healing qualities, and to say to themselves, for instance, "Breathing in, I calm my whole body. Breathing out, I calm my whole body," or "Breathing in, I observe the disappearance of desire. Breathing out, I observe the disappearance of desire."

Vietnamese Zen master Thich Nhat Hanh elaborates on these breath practices with simple natural images: "Breathing in, I see myself as a mountain. Breathing out, I feel solid." "Breathing in, I see myself as space. Breathing out, I feel free."

Light is another image commonly used with breath. Meditators imagine inhaling a pure, energizing light and infusing their entire body with it, or else breathing light directly into a difficult or overwhelming emotion. Sometimes a meditator might also imagine some difficult emotion as a dark cloud, or polluted air being exhaled with each breath.

Tibetan Buddhist teachers such as Tulku Thondup advise us to call on the images of earth, air, fire, water, or space to help us transform emotions. Fire has the power to transform, burn away, or refine. Water is soothing and purifying. Air can sweep in, clean out, and inspire. Earth has the power to stabilize and strengthen. Space gives perspective, lightness, room to move. All of these elements can be invoked or visualized to help us explore and transform emotions.

Of all the elemental images in Tibetan practices, light has the most power when it comes to emotional healing. In the esoteric Tibetan Buddhist teachings, all reality is considered an expression of light; energy and vitality are synonymous with light. In some exercises, meditators visualize balls of light or streams of light pouring down into their bodies; light can be inhaled and circulated through every cell of the body, cleansing and purifying; light can be visualized entering the dark, restricted places in the mind and body; light can be seen awakening us.

Next time you find yourself in a painful emotional state, or even in a mild condition of restlessness or irritation, try working with some of these techniques. Name the emotion, feel it in the body, give it a shape or color or character, and then experience and explore it. Breathe into the feeling that has arisen. Imagine the breath carrying with it light or oceanic calm or whatever image of healing or soothing works for you.

CHAPTER SEVEN

>>> <<<

The Fourth Foundation of Mindfulness

Thinking about Thinking

We are what we think.
All that we are arises with our thoughts.
With our thoughts we make the world.

THE BUDDHA, THE DHAMMAPADA

The Fourth Foundation of Mindfulness may be the trickiest to look at and attend to, because now we are turning the mind upon itself, using the faculty of knowing to examine the faculty of knowing. At this point in our evolutionary journey we are focusing on the uniquely human processes of cognition and conceptualization, standing back (so to speak) to see how consciousness, sensations, reactions, emotions, and thinking all arise and interact with each other. In the *Mahasatipatthana Sutra,* the Fourth Foundation is called *dhammanupassana,* literally translated as "meditation on mind-objects," which includes all of the elements of our experience as set forth in the Buddha's teaching. While the Third Foundation examined our states of mind, the Fourth Foundation looks at how those states are produced, and how we might gain more freedom over that process.

Beginning meditators are often shocked to realize that they can actually observe and investigate their own mental life. Equally astounding to many is the fact that cognition can go on without them, taking care of this or that business, interpreting and reacting in habitual ways to whatever experience registers in awareness. Seeing more clearly into how the mind functions tends to shatter some of the meditator's most cherished beliefs about cognition, consciousness, and the nature of self.

As Tibetan teacher Tulku Urgyen Rinpoche states:

The stream of thoughts surges through the mind of an ordinary person. Often called "black diffusion," this state is an unwholesome pattern of dissipation in which there is no knowledge whatsoever about who is thinking, where the thought comes from, and where the thought disappears. One has not even caught the "scent" of awareness; there are only unwholesome thought patterns operating, so that one is mindlessly carried away by one thought after another. That is definitely not the path of liberation!

Think about your mind for a moment. What is it? How does it function? Does your mind have anything to do with matter? Could you have a mind without a brain? Where exactly is your mind? And what exactly does it do?

For all of our sophisticated understandings about the ways of the world, we remain almost completely ignorant of how what we call "mind" is generated. Most people know more about how coffee is produced than about how their thoughts are created. Most know more about the firing of their automobile engine's pistons than the firing of their brain cells' synapses. People spend more time learning how to reprogram their DVR than learning how to understand their mental habits. If we had any inkling of the problems and suffering that result from our ignorance of and inattention to the workings of our mind, we would immediately drop everything and go on a crash course of intensive meditation.

In general, we live under the illusion that we are in charge of our mind. Sometimes we get a glimpse of the truth, perhaps when we can't stop obsessing about some problem or person, or when we can't stop a barrage of self-criticism. It is only then that we begin to suspect that we may not be the captain of our own ship. After all, if we really were in control of our mind, we could arrange for our memory to always be accurate. If someone told us not to think about a white elephant, we would immediately succeed. If we controlled our mind we could arrange for every fragrance to be beautiful, and all pains—even the important danger signals, after serving their purpose—could be instantly dissolved. If we controlled our mental life, we would be able to turn off our thoughts when they became full of hatred or sorrow, or when they just became repetitive and boring. We could banish all that nasty self-criticism (Why am I such a dunce? Why don't more people love me more?) If we controlled our mind, we could turn off all the worrying and insecurity, the legacy of our biological past that has followed us from the big-fish-eat-little-fish seas and the frightening eat-or-be-eaten forests and savannahs into our societal jungles with their new determinants of success and survival. If we were truly in control of our mind, we would be able to fill it with thoughts of self-worth, love, and happiness, simply at will, all of the time.

In spite of the evidence we continue to believe ourselves in charge of our mental life. Furthermore, we regard the mind as a relatively autonomous force in the world. In the West especially, we have long thought of the mind as superior to the rest of creation. Particularly since Descartes we have considered mind as separate from matter, without substance, a kind of free-floating power that hovers somewhere inside us and manages things.

We also regard our mind as that which represents us, containing our special identity—memories, knowledge, skills, attitudes, preferences. Sometimes, in place of mind, people will use the term "consciousness" to refer to their essential self. Consciousness is generally considered to be that quality of the mind that knows, and that also has a sense of itself as the knower. When we say that someone is "unconscious," we believe that he or she is not *there;* nobody's home.

Developments in neuroscience are now challenging many of our cherished notions of mind and consciousness, suggesting that the mind cannot be separated from matter. Rather, what we've been learning is that human cognition and consciousness can both be explained as evolved functions of the brain that have nothing whatsoever to do with some mysterious soul or self. Many are convinced that we may soon clear up all the gray areas of the mind, including our beliefs about ourselves, by looking into "the gray matter."

THE MATTER OF MIND

Why is thought—being a secretion of the brain—more wonderful than gravity [as] a property of matter? It is our arrogance, our admiration of ourselves.

CHARLES DARWIN,
FROM HIS SECRET NOTEBOOKS

One view in the field of neuroscience is that the brain is the creator of the mind. Experts are saying that what we think of as mind and consciousness are nothing more than byproducts of our brain functions, just as walking is a product of moving our legs. The implication is that mind is not so special—a brilliant evolutionary design, for sure—but completely explainable, and not so very different from other survival adaptations. As MIT science professor Marvin Minsky wrote, "Minds are simply what brains do." Putting it another way, neurologist Richard M. Restak says, "The brain has a mind of its own."

Making use of the latest information from biology, physics, chemistry, and psychology, neuroscientists are formulating a revolutionary new understanding of how the human brain perceives and responds to the world. The researchers are looking into our brain with powerful modern technologies, such as magnetic resonance imaging (MRI); high-resolution electroencephalography (EEG); positron emission tomography (PET) scans, which take color-coded pictures of ongoing brain activity; and the superconducting quantum interference device (SQUID), which measures the magnetic field created by the electrical currents of brain cells.

What is becoming increasingly clear from the research is that we are not who we think we are, and, furthermore, that we may not even be doing the thinking. First of all, according to the neuroscientists, our brain produces its interpretations of reality without ever consulting us. Our thoughts and images are created by mental processes that take place beneath conscious awareness, on what science philosopher Daniel Dennett calls the "subpersonal level." The only world that we know—as presented to us by the brain—is always a touched-up photo, a second-hand story, a revised and edited version of the original.

Most neuroscientists believe that we cannot consciously experience how our reality is created because of the astonishing speed and complexity of the process. Current estimates are that the amazing organ inside your skull contains up to one hundred billion brain cells (neurons), all linked to one another through a trillion synaptic connections. Adding up all the possible combinations results in the number ten followed by millions of zeros, creating more cognitive possibilities in your brain than the number of positively charged particles in the known universe. This complexity is what enables you to imagine this complexity.

And that's just the beginning of the complexity. The inconceivable number of brain cells communicate with each other using both chemicals and electricity, with millions of cell-to-cell firings per second throughout the brain. The result is a self-organizing network so fast and adaptive that the human brain has to be considered the greatest wonder in all the world—at least to itself.

One reason for the complexity of the cognitive process is the fact that different bits of our experience are handled by separate agencies of the brain. For instance, if someone's face appears in your line of sight, different agencies of the brain begin to organize themselves in response to that image. The retinal ganglion cells pick up the contrasts of light and dark to generate a rough representation of the face. The neurons in the primary visual cortex respond to the lines or edges in the image, while other sets of neurons pick up the movement of the image and still others respond to the features of the face and whether or not it is friendly or familiar; at the same time other sets of neurons are preparing to initiate movement or speech in regard to the image. You will become fully conscious of the face only after the brain has made a lot of determinations and decisions for you, and your smile or dismissal may turn out to be little more than a brain-jerk reaction.

In their book *The Embodied Mind,* scientists Francisco Varela, Evan Thompson, and Eleanor Rosch explain that each separate agency or subsystem of the brain "operates only in its local environment," taking care of its own particular task. The new imaging technology reveals that brain functions are so compartmentalized that loud sounds and quiet sounds are handled in different subsectors, and the colors red and green will provoke responses in different parts of the visual cortex. The verbal areas of the brain are so specialized that nouns get processed by different assemblies of neurons than verbs. Furthermore, one group apparently processes regular verbs such as "walk" and "walked," while another processes irregular verbs such as "leap" and "leapt."

What the brain pictures reveal is that our reality is created by many discrete procedures, each of which seem to be operating according to rudimentary principles of stimulus-response. What we have considered so special about us—the ability to conceptualize, reason, find meaning, make fine distinctions and varied responses—appears to be based on the simplest laws of nature. What gives the brain its seemingly magical abilities is the fact that those simple laws are acting across a system of such enormous complexity.

The billions of cells inside the brain remain in a continual resonating communication with each other, perhaps accounting for the proverbial "buzzing" of brains. It's as though all parts of the brain are on a conference call, with every single moment of experience going through multiple reviews and alterations, until all parties come to some mutual agreement. Although it appears to work in a modular and sequential fashion to some degree, the brain is also a parallel processing system.

So far, the scientists cannot find a particular brain region that gives out orders. Every part of the brain knows what every other part of the brain is doing, and each part influences all the others through a type of "dependent co-arising." According to the authors of *The Embodied Mind,* "The behavior of the whole system resembles a cocktail party conversation much more than a chain of command."

In fact, the neuroscientists say your reality is primarily a creation of the brain talking to itself. Nobel laureate Gerald M. Edelman reported that the majority of brain cells are not affected directly by the external world, but only by other brain cells. In an act of seeing, for instance, only 20 percent of the information being processed comes from the retina, while 80 percent comes from other parts of the brain. That means that our perception is four-fifths projection! What you see is not what you get. What you see with your eyes gets passed through millions of years' worth of survival considerations and the memories of all your past experiences in life—and *that's* what you get.

In general, the neuroscientific research indicates that our mental life is a self-adjusting, organic process that goes on without us. The brain seems to be designed by evolution to work so well on our behalf that our presence is not required. We are discovering that what we each call "my" mind is primarily run by nature. And, presumably, nature is doing the best it can for us.

The revolutionary discoveries about the brain's cognitive processes are not such shocking news to those who practice insight meditation. Although it might sound preposterous to some, the path of meditation can reveal the most basic qualities of cognition and consciousness without the use of either MRIs or CAT scans. Evidence of the meditators' understanding is contained in the earliest Buddhist texts and has been confirmed by millions of people in many different cultures throughout history. It's not that meditators are unusually wise or specially chosen to see this. They have simply learned *how* to see it.

> *The purpose of calming the mind in Buddhism is not to become absorbed but to render the mind able to be present with itself long enough to gain insight into its own nature and functioning.*
>
> FRANCISCO VARELA, *THE EMBODIED MIND*

As a simple experiment, close your eyes for a few minutes and simply observe the activities of your brain and nervous system. Do not *intentionally* produce any single thought or sense impression, but instead just let yourself become a neutral, uninvolved witness to what is taking place. You may hear random sounds from the environment registering in your consciousness or hear whispers of thought taking place in the back of your mind, or feel various sensations in your body, or see mental images flash into view.

Simply be aware of whatever impressions pass through your consciousness and notice how your mind reacts to what happens. What triggers a thought? Does your mind automatically identify and name the random sounds that are heard (car engine, dog barking, distant radio)? What moves your attention from one place to another—from thought to sound to physical sensation? Can you count how many different conscious impressions or events take place in one minute? Why does the mind keep working without your willing it to do so?

Although you may not be able to experience the most elementary brain cell activity, in a simple exercise like this you will begin to become more familiar with the self-regulating processes that create your reality.

You may begin to notice the constant monitoring, naming, interpreting, adjusting, and reacting that goes on within you and without *you*. For many people, peering into their mind for the first time—as a neutral witness rather than as a concerned participant or active thinker—can be a major revelation.

> *Just as we walk without thinking, we think without thinking!*
>
> MARVIN MINSKY, *THE SOCIETY OF MIND*

THE BUDDHA BRAIN

The early Buddhist sages explained their understanding of cognition and consciousness in the *Abhidhamma,* introduced in the section on mind-states. Although the details are somewhat different, the sages drew a model of our mental life that is surprisingly similar to that of the neuroscientists. Using only their powers of concentration and mindfulness the sages were able to see the incredible speed of the cognition process, how compartmentalized and segmented it is, and the fact that most of it goes on beneath conscious awareness.

First of all, the Buddhist sages saw that their mental life was fragmented, composed of infinitesimal units of experience that they called mind-moments. The *Abhidhamma* explains that these mind-moments appear and disappear in sequence, almost like energy quanta, and that each mind-moment lasts for only a tiny fraction of the time it takes to blink an eye. Do you have any sense that your mental processes are working at anything near that speed?

The Buddhist "researchers" discovered as well that cognition is not a single event but rather a process composed of many separate segments, something like a mental assembly line for reality. For instance, every experience includes the seven "universal" mental functions of contact, perception, feeling, volition, singleness of object, psychic life, and attention.

Added to that mix will be "nonuniversal" mental factors, which we discussed earlier as influencing mind-states. These arise in response to a particular experience as it happens to a particular person. The non-universal factors include neutral responses such as interest or perplexity, motivations to action such as diligence, hesitancy, or confidence, as well as full-blown mind-states such as anger, elation, or worry. The nonuni-versal factors that appear with some regularity can be considered the habits of our particular mind—our mind's "personality."

The *Abhidhamma* explains that it takes at least seventeen mind-moments for a single cognitive event to complete itself. If the sense-object (sound, smell, thought, etc.) lacks adequate force or interest to the mind, the duration of the cognitive process might last for only fif-teen mind-moments, meaning that full engagement with the object may not occur. Even less intensity might eliminate any conscious awareness or recognition of the object whatsoever.

This map of cognition drawn from the meditations of the early Buddhist sages has striking similarities to the one revealed by the neuroscientists' instruments. To begin with, the sages detailed the phe-nomenal speed and complexity of mental processes, far beyond what the ordinary mind would notice. More specifically, the Buddhists' universal mental factors could be seen as roughly analogous to the neuroscientists' different agencies of the brain, each one taking care of a particular seg-ment of cognition. Meanwhile, the Buddhists' nonuniversal mental factors could be considered equivalent to the patterns of brain cell con-nections that the scientists say become established through a combina-tion of genetic, familial, social, and environmental influences.

One significant difference between the findings of neuroscientists and Buddhist meditators is that while the former may have discovered that our cognitive process goes on largely beneath our conscious aware-ness, the latter reveal that it does not necessarily have to stay that way. It could be said that the scientists have also proven that the human brain can see into its own functioning, albeit with high-powered technology.

But the meditator sees into his or her own cognition process, and therefore the insights have a liberating impact. (Perhaps neuroscientists could offer a valuable aid to spiritual liberation by setting up facilities where each of us could get hooked up to those fancy machines and watch detailed, color pictures of our very own cognitive processes in action—in slow motion, of course.)

Anyone who sits down to meditate, even for short periods of time, will see the truth for themselves. The first crack in the veil of illusion is becoming conscious of how unconscious we normally are. Then, as meditators watch the ordinary functions of mind taking place on their own, they begin to develop a different relationship to their mental life. They can see the evolutionary roots of the mind, and how much of their thinking is spun by Nature's hand. The reactive thought patterns and impulses begin to have less power over them, less ability to mesmerize, capture, and carry them away. Those who meditate still believe in their plans and ideas, and even try to carry them out with passion and zeal, but they may not take the whole business quite so personally. As one saying goes, "To see the mind is to free the mind." To put it another way—seeing is relieving.

> *The disciple Hui-K'e asked Bodhidharma, "Please help me to quiet my mind." Bodhidharma said, "Bring me your mind so that I can quiet it." After a moment Hui-K'e said, "But I can't find my mind." "There," said Bodhidharma, "I have now quieted your mind."*
>
> CHARLES LUK,
> *CHAN AND ZEN TEACHINGS*

CHANGING YOUR MIND

Nature has given all life the ability to learn and change. The neuroscientists support that notion, having discovered that our brain can indeed adapt to new situations. What is surprising is that it seems to do so *all by itself*—the brain appears to be able to change its own mind.

The brain's ability to alter itself is called "self-organizing." Systems theorists describe this ability as a unique feature of living systems, which are flexible, or "open," meaning that they have the power to adapt themselves to changing circumstances. Living systems can develop new forms and functions—new appendages, coloration, mating habits, tools—called "emergent properties," and thereby escape the laws of entropy and increasing disorder. The self-organizing ability of living systems is the sine qua non of evolution.

The neuroscientists say that the brain changes by reconfiguring its "resonating neuronal ensembles"—the patterns of brain cell connections that are established by both evolutionary DNA and early life experiences, the regular paths that stimuli take through our brains to produce pictures of the world and our responses to them. These pathways are usually well developed by early childhood, but if they become unproductive or life-threatening the brain can forge new trails. Based on the perceived requirements of survival or even satisfaction, the brain can develop new resonating neuronal assemblies, reconfiguring its stimulus-response patterns.

One theory, outlined in *The Embodied Mind,* is that the brain changes by reflecting an external model. In this process, the brain cells realign themselves to minimize the difference between their current resonance pattern and what is required in order to be coherent with the model. It is interesting to note that recent educational theories claim that most learning in early childhood—when the brain's neural patterns are still quite flexible—happens when a child models the behavior and attitudes of the most significant people in his or her life.

No matter what we are learning, one particular section of our brain seems to be of utmost importance in bringing about changes in the brain's overall patterning and responses. It should come as no surprise to meditators that this part of the brain is closely associated with focusing attention.

Using PET scans, neuroscientists Michael Posner and Marcus Raichle have done extensive studies on the brain region known as the anterior attentional network, also called "the executive network" because of its apparent importance in making decisions. In their book *Images of Mind,* Posner and Raichle report that the anterior attentional network comes into play when one of several competing meanings or decisions is presented to the brain, and especially if it is called upon to respond in a nonhabitual way. In an exercise called the Stroop Test, for instance, the words for different colors are written out in ink of another color (for example, the word "green" is printed out in red ink), and then the subject is told to ignore the word and name the color of the ink instead. In this test, the anterior attentional network becomes active, inhibiting the more automatic tendency to read the word rather than to regard the color of the ink.

This test, along with several others, suggests that the anterior attentional network is activated when the brain is called upon to focus attention and ignore or alter old neuronal patterns. This could be a different way to describe what is taking place in the practice of mindfulness meditation.

In Buddhist practices, mindfulness is considered one of the most important of all the mental factors because it has the unique ability to intervene in the cognitive process. When mindfulness is engaged it brings an intensified awareness to what is taking place in the mind and can suspend the habitual reactions. Old mental patterns can be weakened and new options created. Consequently, Buddhist meditation teachers place great emphasis on developing the mindfulness factor and applying its power to all aspects of our being. It would be interesting to research—perhaps with MRIs and EEGs—whether mindfulness is somehow associated with the anterior attentional network. Perhaps when people are engaged in mindfulness meditation, this executive network is lit up with activity.

Zen Master Ikkyu was asked by a disciple for some wisdom to live by. The master wrote on a piece of paper, "Attention." After reading this message the disciple asked, "Couldn't you offer something more?" Ikkyu took back the paper and wrote, "Attention. Attention." Again the disciple asked for something more, and Ikkyu again took back the paper. This time he wrote, "Attention. Attention. Attention." The disciple bowed deeply and departed.

THE CASE OF THE MISSING PERSONS
Part I

The issue of changing the brain's cognitive patterns or the habits of the mind brings us to a core question for both Buddhist sages and scientists alike: who or what is doing the changing? Is there a region of the brain or a mental factor that is in charge of the entire process? And if not, then why do we always have this feeling that *someone* is initiating and directing the activities of our mind? How and why and where does this sense of "self" fit into the process?

After examining the cognitive process with all of their sophisticated scans and scopes, current research can't seem to locate the self, the one who directs the show. They know, for instance, that knowing is going on, but they can't figure out who or what is doing the knowing, and where it resides. Neuroscientists are searching through the passageways of the brain, calling out, "Take me to your leader!" But nobody is answering back.

Nearly three decades ago, *Time* magazine summarized the latest brain research in a cover story entitled "In Search of the Mind." Most people were probably not aware that the mind was lost, and chances are they became quite disturbed to discover that even the neuroscientists couldn't find it.

The *Time* article concluded, "Despite our every instinct to the contrary, consciousness is not some entity inside the brain, march up the optic nerve, round and round the cortex, looking behind every neuron, and then before you know it, you emerge into daylight on the spike of a motor nerve impulse, scratching your head and wondering where the self is."

Of course, we will all object strongly to the denial of our existence, and there are plenty of arguments we can make. (Based on the studies of cognition, however, we should probably forget about *cogito ergo sum*.) But isn't it possible that we're looking for the self in the wrong place? As disciples of the seventeenth-century Enlightenment, they would naturally conclude that if they can't find the self in our brain then it "simply does not exist." Remember—heads are us.

Perhaps the scientists should have also looked in the heart organ, where Aristotle believed the mind to reside, or even in the liver, which some cultures believe houses the core of self. And couldn't it also be possible that consciousness exists in every cell of our body, or that—to steal a concept from quantum physics—consciousness is nonlocal? Perhaps consciousness has no material base at all, and the neuroscientists' search for the seat of self will end up just like the physicists' search for an elementary particle: at the core they will find a process rather than a thing.

> *When we examine all that we call mind, we see only a conglomeration of mental elements, not a self. Feeling, memory, perception, are all shifting through the mind like leaves in the wind. We can discover this through meditation.*
>
> AJAHN CHAH,
> *A STILL FOREST POOL*

THE CASE OF THE MISSING PERSONS
Part II

Anyone who studies the mind will eventually come to the "hard problem" of consciousness, and Buddhist meditators are no exception. The hard problem in consciousness, first posed by David Chalmers, posits that we can describe the physical mechanisms of the brain in exact detail, down to the neuron, but that description of a physical state has no explanatory power over why there is a such thing as a mental state. One could describe every neuron every second involved in the process of recognizing a face, but that can never explain why it's *like something* to recognize that face. That inability to explain why is what Chalmers termed the hard problem. In Chalmers' view, the impossibility means that neuroscientists, psychologists, and others need to turn to a non-physical explanation for conscious experience.

For nearly three millennia, meditators have been looking through their minds and bodies for a "self" they could call their own, or for the essence or locale of consciousness. And like the neuroscientists, they have come up scratching their heads and wondering where it could be. The conclusion that many have arrived at, summarized by Buddhist scholar Walpola Rahula in his classic book *What the Buddha Taught* is that "what we call 'I' or 'being' is only a combination of physical and mental aggregates, which are working together interdependently in a flux of momentary change within the law of cause and effect." Hardly what you might consider a religious or even "spiritual" viewpoint.

In the *Abhidhamma,* however, the Buddhist sages are teaching that consciousness is not some mystical essence of the soul or spirit, but rather a natural occurrence, what systems theorists call an "emergent property" of human life. The sages came to this view after observing their own minds in meditation and realizing that the nature of consciousness is actually quite different than our ordinary experience of it.

Meditators are often surprised, for instance, when they notice that consciousness is not continuous. With the application of mindfulness, they begin to see that, rather than a permanent "knower" or a steady-state condition, consciousness can be seen to arise anew in every split second or mind-moment. We normally don't see this segmented quality of our knowing because the process is taking place so quickly.

A very simple experiment can reveal the fragmented nature of consciousness. Stop reading for a moment and look intently at some stationary object. Maintaining the visual sense impression, notice if you can *simultaneously* hear sounds. Can you be conscious of seeing and hearing at the same time? If you pay very close attention you might notice consciousness switching back and forth from eye to ear with great rapidity. While we seem to experience multiple sense impressions as a single conscious event, it is a false effect created by the speed of the cognitive process. The real question here, of course, is whether you can be *conscious* of walking and chewing gum at the same time.

According to the Buddha's teachings, there are actually six different types of consciousness, each one associated with a particular sense door. Only when something is seen does "eye-consciousness" arise, and only when there is a thought will "thinking-consciousness" be present. In the words of the Buddha, "Consciousness is defined according to the condition through which it arises. . . . If it is conditioned by eye and material objects, it is called eye-consciousness . . . if through mind and mental objects, mind-consciousness." Each type of consciousness will appear only in conjunction with an object—a sight, sound, taste, smell, touch, or thought. In other words, consciousness does not exist independent of its function, and there is not *one* consciousness.

In Buddhist psychology, seeing the discontinuity of consciousness is a somewhat commonplace breakthrough in self-awareness. Meditators begin to realize that even consciousness has no separate, independent existence, but is always co-arising with its object. Accompanying this insight, the meditators may also begin to understand themselves as co-emergent with the world.

> *When we see how the seemingly simplest process of consciousness proves to be a most complicated collaboration of innumerable elements . . . which cannot be regarded as the expression of an ego-substratum, but in which, on*

the contrary, the ego-idea arises as a product of certain functions—then a further cornerstone of the Buddhist doctrine is revealed: the idea of anatta (non-self).

LAMA GOVINDA, *THE PSYCHOLOGICAL ATTITUDE OF EARLY BUDDHIST PHILOSOPHY*

At the core of the Buddha's teaching of liberation is the concept of non-self, or *anatta*. This is often misunderstood as some kind of nihilistic doctrine that says you and I don't exist in any sense of the word. Instead, the Buddha was teaching that our lives are a play of natural elements and processes, that there is no independently existing self apart from all of biological and cosmic evolution. The Buddha realized that by experiencing this truth inside us, we can weaken our inordinate attachment to our individual drama, relieve our suffering, and increase our compassion for all life.

Sometimes the doctrine of non-self is explained as "ultimate" truth in contrast to the "relative" truth of our separate, individual lives where we each have name, form, and social security number. In Buddhist teachings, when the term "self" is used in its ultimate, phenomenological sense it refers to something that is singular or "uncompounded," which means that its existence does not depend on the coming together of any two separate elements and, furthermore, that it will be able to sustain itself independently from all other things. That definition of self would certainly eliminate a human body and mind. In its ultimate meaning, an existing self would also have to be unchanging, and therefore not subject to the laws of physics or biology. Certainly no one that you or I know would fit that description.

By any of these criteria, all things, including human beings, can be said to be without self. In fact, all things can be said to be without ultimate "thingness." This is the basis for the common Buddhist notion of the emptiness of the world. All that we know of in nature is compounded, conditioned, and in process, and therefore is empty or devoid of any ultimate selfhood. Quantum physics and evolutionary biology are the modern scientific proof of that. Mindfulness meditation is the ultimate personal test of these ultimate truths.

Meanwhile, throughout the Pali Canon the Buddha and his disciples make many references to individuals and persons, without any sense of violating the doctrine of ultimate non-self. Furthermore, most Buddhist teachings are based on the idea that *someone* can meditate, that *someone* can awaken, and that *someone* has enough personal freedom to develop mindfulness and see right through his or her someonehood. The Buddha consistently emphasized the precious quality of a human birth, because only as a human can we recognize our true nature and relieve our suffering.

The sense of self itself is perfectly natural. All forms of life must have some boundaries. Even the one-celled organism has a membrane that outlines its being. Our current complex self-identification may well be an evolved outgrowth of that single cell's outer membrane. Furthermore, our own boundary is just as thin and transparent as that of a cell. Just by looking closely we can see right through it.

The Buddha's teaching shows us how to see through our relative boundaries into the ultimate truth of what Thich Nhat Hanh calls our "interbeing." As meditators move through the Four Foundations of Mindfulness, they begin to see clearly that the self we carry around is not self-created nor self-sustaining; nothing about you or me can be isolated from the earth, the atmosphere, or the natural processes of life itself. Meditators also come to realize that our mental and emotional life is woven around archetypal, species-wide patterns of reaction, and the more closely this is seen, the harder it becomes to identify those patterns as "I" or "mine." The practice of meditation is not to see that we are nothing, but to see that every moment of our experience is part of great currents of life and energy, built out of multiple elements and conditions from both the past and present, internal and external, far and near. We begin to realize that we exist only in relationship, and that rather than being nothing, we could more accurately say that we are everything. We co-exist and dependently co-arise with all creation. This realization is the fruit of meditation practice, best expressed by the great Zen master Dogen: "To study Buddhism is to study the self. To study the self is to know the self. To know the self is to forget the self. And to forget the self is to become one with all the things of the world."

EXERCISES

❧ Mind Games ❧

Following are some specific exercises that can be used to conduct an active investigation into the nature of your mind. Any of these exercises can be used either in conjunction with or independent from a regular course of meditation practice. In my teaching experience, I have found that these meditations and reflections can lead people to profound insights, even if the exercises are done only a few times.

An important thing to remember when playing the mind games is to be gentle with yourself, and not to judge too harshly what you will observe in your mind. Be assured that your lack of mental control or confusion is a common, species-wide condition.

A second important point to remember is that these meditation exercises are not about getting rid of our thoughts. This notion is one of the most common mistakes of beginning meditators. There are indeed times when a determined attempt at blocking thoughts can be useful, such as in the development of concentration, but a mind empty of thoughts is not the goal. Not only would it be an unnatural condition, but furthermore, if we *could* actually get rid of all our thoughts in meditation we would never get to see how our ordinary mind functions.

One useful way to regard your thinking is to recognize it as a natural occurrence. See if you can view thinking as a pulse similar to your breathing or heartbeat, a vital part of existence—with all of its attendant difficulties—gifted to you by evolution. Then you can begin to explore your mental life as a scientist of the self, applying mindfulness to this amazing natural phenomenon.

Thought Happens!

The first exercise is very simple. Just sit down and close your eyes, and for the next ten minutes make the firm intention not to think a single thought or give rise to a single mental image. You can either try to focus on your breath as a place to put your mind, or just sit there.

During the ten minutes, notice if any thoughts appear in your mind. If they do, remember that they appeared independent of your conscious will or direction. If some thoughts do appear, and they probably will, this will be your first clue. You have just seen that *your* thinking can go on without *you*. After all, you had vowed not to think for ten minutes, and thoughts came anyway. Who was doing the thinking?

If you did go for a full ten minutes without one thought appearing in your mind, you are a freak of human nature. For most people, thoughts and images will appear many times in a ten-minute period, all by themselves.

One of the most shocking insights for beginning meditators is this realization that they are not necessarily generating their own mental life. The more one meditates, the deeper this insight penetrates, and the harder it is to find "the thinker." The more deeply one sees into the cognition process, the more shocking it can become, and also the more liberating.

The next time you do this exercise, try taking the simple vow—as strange as it may sound—to *not* think about your thoughts. If a thought arises, be determined not to analyze it or cogitate over it, but simply to notice that a thought has occurred, and then let it go. You might think of each appearance of thought as a "thought event." Just watch the blips of thought appear and disappear. You are learning to be an observer of your own mind.

Listen, Do You Want to Know a Secret?

For this mind game, simply listen to yourself thinking. In mystical writings you may have heard about developing a third eye or wisdom eye. In this exercise you can develop a third ear. And then eavesdrop on yourself.

For this exercise to be revealing, you should plan to sit for fifteen or twenty minutes at least. After closing your eyes and centering your awareness on the breath, simply turn your hearing toward whatever thoughts arise. Listen to your mind as it monitors the world, worries over your future, judges your success or failures. Listen to your mind talking to itself, always going on about something.

After you listen for a while, see if you can sharpen the focus of your inner ear, so that you catch the very first hint of a thought or image. Listen for the beginning whispers of thought, or even the initial impulse to think.

As you begin to catch your thoughts earlier in their creation, see if you can just *let them go* before they complete themselves. Practice allowing thoughts to occur without identifying them as yours, analyzing or judging them, or believing in their significance. Don't worry that you might die or completely come apart during this exercise. Remember that you are simply investigating your mind, and that it will quite readily return to "normal" functioning.

You might also listen for the almost imperceptible whispers of thought that often play through the back recesses of your mind. Can you hear all those thoughts that might have gone on almost beneath consciousness? Thoughts that might have died as minor impulses or instincts?

The Name Game

The practice of naming or labeling—as introduced in the section on mind-states—can be very helpful as we examine cognition as well. When we give each thought a simple category—"planning thought," "judging thought," "regretting thought"—it helps us to be a neutral observer. The process of labeling relaxes our identification with our thinking, and therefore weakens our habitual reactions. We are actually gaining enough distance from the thought to notice its ancestry and characteristics. Labeling will reveal what kind of thoughts predominate in our minds, and also how those thoughts are related to certain primal motivations or tendencies.

To begin the practice of labeling, take a few meditation periods, and as thoughts appear in the mind simply give them a silent mental label, such as "thoughts" or "thinking." After you become familiar with this technique, you can get more specific with the labels. For instance, you might categorize a thought or group of thoughts as "planning," "worrying," or "analyzing."

The practice of naming is like becoming a biologist of the mind, classifying the flora and fauna that come into view and noticing how they are related to each other in the ecosystem. You are not specifically looking for anything, but simply noting what occurs and which species predominate.

Remember, you have permission to be creative in these meditation exercises. They are not sacred ritual. Go ahead and give personal or even funny names to your thought clusters, or find new ways of dividing them into categories.

Grounds for Thought

Just as we did with mind states, if we look closely we will find that most of our thoughts can also be seen as an extension or elaboration of some primal energy. We can explore this phenomenon by categorizing and labeling our thoughts according to their simplest motivations. In this way we can examine the relationship of our thinking to both instinct and ego. During the course of several meditation sessions, begin to notice and label your thoughts according to some of the following categories:

Staying Alive. How many of your thoughts have something to do with your physical survival? You could put all of your worrying and planning thoughts in this category: rehearsing the future, concerns about health or money, family, job, time pressures, global disasters. Remember that worrying is perfectly normal, and therefore you need not worry about how much you worry. It's just your survival brain trying to protect you, working overtime.

The "I"-"Me"-"Mine" Mind. The real true love of my mind is me. It is always thinking of me, always trying to do the best it knows how for me. Your mind is probably doing the same for you. (Even our self-judgment is a survival tactic, a bitter pill.) Take a few meditation periods to explore how much of your thinking revolves around your image of yourself, your status in the family, the community, the world.

Here Come da Judge. Take one entire meditation session and count the number of self-judgments that occur. Many people are astounded to discover how poorly they are thought of by their own mind. Take another session and notice how many of your thoughts are judgments about anything and everything. In a competitive world we have to continually judge and compare to know where we stand and to figure out our chances for success.

Chasing the Train

During a normal twenty or thirty-minute meditation period, the mind is bound to wander off the breath. Some thought or feeling is sure to lure us into its web and carry us off into another reality. This exercise is designed to examine the nature of these entanglements.

Close your eyes and bring awareness to the sensations of breath. During the meditation period, whenever you discover that you are lost in thought, just stop for a few minutes, and trace back the sequence of thoughts that you just went through. See if you can find the connections, the place where one thought or group of thoughts triggered another. Notice also if there is any theme to the thoughts. Do they all relate to a particular mood or mind-state?

To play these mind games, it helps to do regular daily half-hour meditations for a number of weeks or months. That way you can slowly shift the theme of the exercises and give yourself a thorough mental checkup. After you become more familiar with these various techniques, it also gets easier and easier to observe your thoughts rather than being lost in them.

You may be surprised at the shift that occurs after playing just a few of the mind games. You might find that you are much more aware of the process and content of your thoughts, and that you are developing a somewhat different relationship toward thinking in general. The mind games tend to reverberate through your life, even after you have stopped playing or forgotten about them. Suddenly you may remember the meditation perspective and catch your mind off guard. Inadvertently sneaking up on it in this way can be very revealing, and often somewhat embarrassing.

THE MIND BEHIND THE MIND

The wisdom-mind of all the Buddhas, innate wakefulness,
is inherent to our very nature, yet it is temporarily obscured
by conceptuality.

NYOSHUL KHENPON, *NATURAL GREAT PERFECTION*

Many Buddhist sages seem to be having a love affair with the mind. They know that it is Nature's most precious gift, and that it will serve us well to explore all of its possibilities and dimensions.

In contrast to the scientists who consider the mind to be a by-product of the brain, there are many Buddhists who conclude that the brain is actually a by-product of mind. This idea, sometimes called the "mind only" view, holds that all phenomena are mental creations.

As the Shabkar Lama, a famous Tibetan Buddhist mystic of the seventeenth century wrote, in *The Flight of the Garuda,* "The mind is like an artist. The body is created by mind, as are all the many worlds existing in the three dimensions of microcosmic world systems: all of them are also drawn by the mind."

Modern science would find some agreement with that statement. Although scientists do not attribute any mystical quality to our minds, they do acknowledge that the brain and nervous system construct our reality. Nature has no inherent color, sound, touch, smell, or feel. As psychologist Robert Ornstein wrote, "The outside world is silent and dull of itself." Furthermore, by looking through microscopes, telescopes, and other measuring devices, scientists have learned that our ordinary mind sees a particular dimension and frequency of reality. When it comes to simple perception, the mind is always at least co-creating our particular world.

Some Buddhist schools also talk reverently about a universal Mind (often spelled with a capital *M*) that is like a substrate or ground of being. This universal Mind is variously described as "luminous," "immaculate," "lucid," "unstained," and "ineffable." Over the centuries, the universal Mind has been given many wondrous names, including *the unborn, the source, the predicateless primordial essence, the weaver of the web of appearances,* and—a breathless Tibetan Buddhist appellation—the *out-breather and the in-breather of infinite universes throughout the endless duration of time.* For some, the universal Mind has godlike attributes: it is the great mystery itself, the creator and destroyer, all-knowing and all-powerful.

Some Buddhist schools teach that we each carry within us the "original mind" or the "true nature" of mind. The twentieth-century Tibetan master Tulku Urgyen describes this nature as "unconfined empty cognizance." In other words, the essence of mind is the pure power of knowing. And, he says, "that which knows is, in essence, empty. It is cognizant by nature, and its capacity is unconfined. Try to see this for yourself."

To picture this true nature of mind, imagine an expanse of clear, empty sky. All phenomena appear and disappear into this sky, such as clouds, birds, planes, or planets, but everything passes through without leaving a trace or mark. Likewise, the sky of mind holds on to nothing, and therefore remains unchanged by sadness or physical pain or the sight of a sunset. The mind's only inherent characteristic is pure knowing, or what some Buddhists refer to as "simple awareness."

This image of mind is useful for meditators, who over the course of practice start to identify more closely with awareness itself than with the phenomena that move through it. I remember a sudden, very liberating shift of perspective when I first began to imagine my essential mind as a calm, spacious sky of knowing. My mind opened to everything that appeared—images, thoughts, sounds, even the torments and ecstasies of my psyche—and saw them all as transient, ultimately unsatisfactory, and as archetypal rather than personal. As many meditators will testify, being in this state of consciousness can provide a deep rest for the mind, as well as offer powerful insights into its nature.

According to the noted twentieth-century Thai Buddhist master Ajahn Chah, the Buddha's awakening began with this look into the nature of mind: "The Buddha saw that whatever the mind gives rise to are just transitory, conditioned phenomena, which are really empty. When this dawned on him, he let go and found an end to suffering. The true nature of mind is free, shining, resplendent. The mind becomes occupied only because it misunderstands and is deluded by these conditioned phenomena, this false sense of self."

As we saw earlier, neuroscience would clearly suggest that the mind (a product of the brain) creates "transitory, conditioned phenomena," and that there is nothing to point to as a single self or agent directing them. Furthermore, in this, all of our perceptions, feelings, and thoughts are based on evolutionary imperatives and therefore lack any independent selfhood. This leads to the "hard problem" of consciousness for the neuroscientists, but to Buddhist meditators working with the Fourth Foundation of Mindfulness it is not a problem at all. In fact, realizing that the core of one's being is not any of the passing mental phenomena but rather this wondrous awareness itself is an extremely liberating insight.

As Buddhist and neuroscientist Francisco Varela wrote in the book *The Embodied Mind,* "Science has shown us that a fixed self is not necessary for mind but has not provided any way of dealing with the basic fact that this no-longer-needed self is precisely the ego-self that everyone clings to and holds most dear."

Meditation is the key. As meditators come to identify themselves with awareness rather than the phenomena that pass through it, they gain a new sense of peace. It becomes clear how the ordinary mind— guided by the ego or the conceit of "I"—is driven here and there by instincts of approach avoidance, aversion and desire, and thereby is continually creating its own suffering. When the mind begins to see its true, empty nature, it starts to relax; it takes a rest from reacting both to the world and to its own creations.

As Zen master Shunryu Suzuki wrote in *Zen Mind, Beginner's Mind,* his classic book on Buddhist practice: "It is when you sit in [meditation] that you will have the most pure, genuine experience of the empty state of mind. 'Essence of mind,' 'original mind,' 'original face,' 'Buddha nature,' 'emptiness'—all these words mean the absolute calmness of our mind."

It is through the process of meditation that we can come to know both the ordinary functioning of the mind and, in contrast, the mind's calm, empty essence. In meditation we see the mind that we inherit from evolution and begin to learn of its true potential. Part of that potential is the capacity for great ease, as well as more love and compassion for all other sentient beings. The other part is the power to gaze directly into the wondrous, magical void, the universal essence that is empty of person, place, or thing.

> *Depth increases from subconscious to self-conscious to superconscious, on the way to its own shocking recognition, utterly one with the radiant All, and we awaken as that oneness.*
>
> KEN WILBER,
> *A BRIEF HISTORY OF EVERYTHING*

EXERCISES

❧ Big Sky Mind Meditations ❧

Some of my favorite meditation practices are variations on what is sometimes called the Big Sky Mind meditation. Making use of the imagination, these exercises can create a very relaxed and spacious feeling in one's mind, while at the same time offering deep insights into how the mind functions. What more could anyone want from a meditation?

Big Sky Seeing

The first Big Sky exercise is done with the eyes open and can be practiced either in a closed space or outside. In a seated position, look straight ahead and let your gaze become very soft and somewhat unfocused. Allow the edges of your vision to extend sideways, upward, and downward, so that you are taking in as much of the scene around you as possible. You have *vista* vision. Remember to let the gaze be unfocused, the eyes soft and relaxed.

Now begin to imagine that consciousness is actually infusing and filling the entire area that you are seeing. The space of pure, clear knowing has expanded in all directions to become as large as the expanse of your vision.

After holding that impression for a few minutes, begin to sense that consciousness is also existing behind, above, and beneath you, *beyond* the area of your vision. Consciousness is now encompassing the space all around you. Consciousness has become identical with that space, receiving and knowing all the objects and phenomena that appear within its expanse. If you are in a room, you might sense that conscious awareness is filling it completely, from floor to ceiling, and wall to wall. Within this space you can feel your body and breath, be aware of thoughts or sounds—all of it arising into this grand space of consciousness. Any movement or sound that happens is taking place within the Big Sky—or Big Room—of mind.

The key to this exercise is to suspend the idea that consciousness is emanating only from your head. Instead feel your head and body *in the middle* of consciousness, as another bundle of phenomena being known or sensed. Holding the feeling of clear, all-pervasive consciousness, let things happen or appear within this space without any interpretation or interference. Within the expanded area of awareness you may feel your body and breath, be aware of thoughts or physical sensations, or the sounds and movements in the environment. Just relax into the Big Sky Mind and let everything happen and disappear on its own.

The above exercise can be especially wonderful when done outside, where it often generates a satisfying and all-encompassing feeling of one-ness with Earth, sky, and the natural environment. In a setting with a big or expansive horizon such as mountains or seashore, the meditator can get a sense of consciousness being almost boundless, truly becoming a Big *Sky* Mind.

When outdoors, let your gaze rest just above the far horizon, keeping the eyes relaxed and unfocused. Begin to sense that your conscious aware-ness is expanding outward in all directions to infuse and encompass the entire natural scene surrounding you. Consciousness is no longer just emanating from your head but is everywhere: in front, above, beneath, and behind you. Slowly let your sense of the edges or boundaries of consciousness dissolve; allow the clear, pure expanse of knowing become coterminous with the space that surrounds the entire Earth, the space that has no boundaries. All movements, sounds, thoughts, physical sensations, people, trees, mountains, oceans, and planets are temporary appearances in the vast expanse of the Big Sky Mind.

> *Live all visual and auditory experience without attachment, as hallucination, dream, the reflection of the moon in water, a fairy palace in the sky, a distortion of Sigh, an apparition, a bubble, and an echo.*
>
> THE SHABKAR LAMA,
> *THE FLIGHT OF THE GARUDA*

Big Sky Hearing

Another version of the Big Sky Mind meditation is done with eyes closed and focuses on sounds as the medium of mind expansion. When we don't try to interpret or identify sounds, they begin to take on a very evanescent quality. The nature of sound itself can reveal impermanence and also bring a great sense of space to the mind. When done outside, this exercise can be especially effective in creating a feeling of integration with the natural world.

Begin in the standard fashion, resting awareness in the breath to establish yourself in meditation. After a few minutes on the breath, bring awareness to your sense of hearing. Become aware of the sounds in your immediate environment. If you are in a house you might hear a clock ticking, the refrigerator motor, the sound of voices coming from another room, or even the sound of cars passing in the street. If you are outdoors you might hear the rustle of wind in trees or grasses, bird calls, human voices, or car or airplane motors.

Let the sounds appear without trying to name or analyze them. Adopt the attitude of *receiving* the sounds as they randomly occur, letting them appear and disappear in your mind. Let this happen with as little effort as possible. Recognize that you don't have to do anything. The sounds will appear on their own, and so will the knowing of them.

Eventually let your conscious awareness extend outward to focus on the more distant sounds you can hear. Perhaps you will become aware of a far-off airplane motor, or the faint sound of thunder, or voices or a radio in the distance. As you hear the more distant sounds, sense or imagine that the edge of your consciousness has extended out as far as the source of the farthest sounds you can hear. Slowly let the edges of consciousness dissolve. Begin to sense that pure, empty awareness extends without limit in all directions. Let consciousness become identical with space itself.

After you have established the expanded sense of Big Sky Mind, just let the sounds appear and disappear in this vast space. Imagine the sounds arising, bubbling up into awareness. Similarly, recognize thoughts, physical sensations, and breath as having the same ephemeral quality as the sounds, appearing and disappearing in the Big Sky of Mind.

To renew the expanded consciousness just bring attention back to the farthest sounds you can hear. As always, before you end the meditation bring your awareness back into the breath for a few minutes, resting in the familiar rhythm.

The Crowd Meditation:
Many Minds in the Big Mind

You can initiate this Big Sky Mind exercise when you are in the presence of other people, either indoors or outside, at a gathering or just walking down the street. Even a few minutes of this practice can create a feeling of ease and acceptance as well as a bond with other people.

Begin by establishing the sense of an expanded field of awareness, as though the boundaries extend far above, below, and all around you and the scene you are witnessing. Next begin to notice the people that are contained in this vast expanse of awareness. Notice them simply through their movement, the sounds they make, their aliveness, their existence as concentrations of energy. As you hold the people within the expanded space of awareness realize that each person's mind is generating his or her own thoughts, impressions, desires, and feelings. Without letting your imagination become too specific, and without judgment, begin to sense all of the contents of these particular minds arising and disappearing into the vast open space. Imagine all of this human mind energy continuously bubbling up into the empty sky. Now include your own thoughts, sensations, and feelings. Sense them appearing and vanishing along with all the others into the vast, open space. Realize that all of these human creations are unique and yet very similar; all of them temporary appearances under the one Big Sky of Mind.

Seeing Between the Lines

Begin this exercise by looking around you for a few minutes and noticing all of the things that you see. Chances are that you will indeed see "things"— chairs, plants, people, lights, walls. Our attention naturally comes to rest on objects, on particulars. That is part of our genius as a species. But hardly anyone who does this exercise for the first time will report seeing space. A few people have mentioned that they see light or color, but space—that which contains and surrounds every little thing—stays hidden to almost everyone's vision.

Now look again and pay attention to the space. Regard the emptiness in between things, and then the big space of the room or the sky.

Although you can't exactly focus on it, begin to examine the qualities of space. For one thing, as you look around at space, notice how much bigger it is than everything else. There is more space in the universe than anything.

Also notice the function of space. One purpose it serves is to keep things from bumping into each other. In fact, without space there wouldn't be things. Just one big lump. Recognize that if you knock down the walls of a room, the space will still be there. If you take the things away, space will take their place. (Although we know the space that we are looking at is full of molecules, it is relatively empty, at least empty enough to give us a simulated experience of *real* space.)

As you examine space, begin to feel it all around you. Spend a few minutes just experiencing yourself in space. Feel yourself inside it, embraced by it. Turn your head or move your arm and feel it moving through space. The next time you take a walk feel your entire body moving through space.

After experiencing the space all around you for a few minutes, also start to sense its existence very high above and below you. To enhance this part of the exercise, become aware of yourself on the Earth. Remember that the Earth is like a spaceship, and we are all riding on it through vast expanses of space.

When you have a chance, you can get a wondrous new perspective on space by lying down on your back outside, in a place where your view of sky is unobstructed. Then begin to imagine that you are looking *downward* into space. This has as much validity as the notion that you are looking up. Space has no bottom, top, or sides.

I heard a figure that might help you reflect a little on the space around you. Some ambitious astrophysicists tried to figure out the current size of the universe, and came up with ten billion, trillion, trillion cubic light-years. Sure, why not? And you are somewhere inside that expanse of space, in fact, moving rapidly through it. As you feel yourself on the Earth, you might reflect that the planet is spinning around on its axis at one thousand miles per hour, and around the sun at sixty-six thousand miles per hour. The Solar System is moving through the Milky Way galaxy at the rate of a half million miles per hour, and the entire galaxy is speeding at nearly a million miles an hour toward a point in interstellar space known as the Great Attractor. And, yes, everything attracted to the Great Attractor is traveling at nearly another million miles an hour toward another supercluster of galaxies called the Shapely Attractor. Hmmmm?

Although we can't actually experience this movement through space, the reflection at least offers us a dose of wonder, if not humility. The important aspect of the exercise, however, is to have a sense or experience of that most neglected element of our lives—space.

Spaceheads

We will now switch this space exercise to our own minds. Just as you looked around you with your eyes open and then named what you saw, now close your eyes and look around at what arises in your awareness. You may have gotten a hint from the above exercise, but if not, chances are what you will report seeing in your mind are "things." You would naturally notice thoughts, images, sounds, perhaps flickering light, maybe some physical sensations. But do you notice the space in which it all occurs? Call it empty cognizance, or field of awareness, or simply space—this is the expanse into which your world unfolds.

Try to become aware of just the space in your mind. You might imagine this mind space as a Big Sky, or a field of pure knowing, or a mirror-like expanse that reflects anything that passes before it. You may not be able to actually focus on this reflecting or knowing space, but you can sense its presence. Recognize that every sound, thought, and feeling is taking place in this calm, empty expanse of awareness.

Try this exercise several times, and for longer and longer periods. See if you can feel that your true self is that calm, knowing space in your mind. Just sit and watch all of the other phenomena appear and disappear through this space. Because you are not identified with the mental phenomena, you can let them all come and go with ease. By taking your focus off the objects in your mind, you might begin to get a different view of who you really are. Play with this new sense of yourself. Relax and enjoy the show.

✺ ✺

Evolving
toward Enlightenment

*This is the way for the purification of beings, for the
overcoming of sorrow and lamentation, for the destroying of
pain and grief, for reaching the right path, for the realization
of Nirvana, namely the Four Foundations of Mindfulness.*

THE BUDDHA, IN THE
MAHASATIPATTHANA SUTRA

After taking an evolutionary journey through the Four
Foundations of Mindfulness, you might now have a somewhat
different answer to the question "Who am I?" Hopefully the meditations and reflections in this book have offered you a larger context for
your life, having placed it within the stream of evolution. As part of
your self-description you might now somehow include the sun's energy
or your skeletal structure; you might acknowledge your nature as air-
breathing or two-legged. At moments of inquiry you might remember
the distant ancestral sources of your current emotions, or feel yourself
part of the history of all life, or even recognize your present experience as being co-emergent with all phenomena through time. Even
when done just a few times, the exercises in this book can begin to
shift our identity beyond our individual personalities to include the

world, increasing our sense of wonder and mystery at the same time.

Although we may never again view ourselves in quite the same way, the initial insights are just the beginning of a course in evolutionary wisdom and are only the first steps on the Buddha's path of self-realization or enlightenment. Unless these insights are gradually deepened and integrated into our lives they will remain abstract knowledge, just another bunch of facts without any power to change our feelings or behavior. As one Korean Zen master put it, we can have "sudden enlightenment," but for that enlightenment to have any impact requires "gradual cultivation."

That's why meditation is called a "practice." Most of us will never get "there," never arrive at a steady state of "happiness ever after" or "perfect wisdom." Nature's odds are against it. Humans seem to be novices at self-realization. And while mindfulness meditation may be an evolutionary sport, like evolution itself the game is never finished. One reason is that if we are indeed evolving, then we will always need remedial training in self-awareness. Looking at history, it does appear as though we are always just barely catching up with where we are going.

That is why we need to practice. If we want to cultivate peace and freedom of mind we have to practice. These qualities do not seem to be our birthright. (Remember, we were born in "original sin"; we inherit *animal* instincts.) If we want to remember our connection with nature or the cosmos, we have to somehow touch those truths regularly, preferably every day. We have to put on our wider perspectives and wear them until they become our most familiar views of the world. We will simultaneously be teaching our ego its new place in the scheme of things. Paraphrasing poet Gary Snyder, meditation is a process of entering into our deep identity over and over again, until it becomes the identity from which we live. So how do you become more enlightened? The same way you get to Carnegie Hall—practice.

It is also important to remember that evolutionary wisdom is not just about learning how to alter reactive habits but is in equal measure about learning to accept ourselves. Sitting in meditation shows us how deep our conditioning goes and prevents us from becoming too idealistic about "evolving." Rome wasn't built in a day, and the modern human condition wasn't built in even a thousand millennia. The habits of the heart and the "resonating neuronal assemblies" are deeply encoded; the stimuli's responses run deep. One of the greatest gifts of evolutionary wisdom is to reveal the primal quality of our neuroses; to show us its inherited, collective, archetypal nature. Self-realization is not some mystical endgame. Knowing who we are also means that we don't kid ourselves about our possibilities. Evolutionary wisdom means that we get real.

If you want to deepen your self-awareness and the effects of the exercises in this book, it is important to establish a regular meditation practice. When we first wake up in the morning is the best time to get in touch with our deep identity. Otherwise, we get immediately caught in the tangled dramas of selfhood and will forget to feel our simple *aliveness.* We will get caught up in all the things we have to accomplish and will live that day without any connection to or appreciation for the air or the planet revolving beneath us, turning us toward the light.

At any time during the day we can place attention on our breath and reflect upon it as the basic pulse of our life, an identity as vital as any goal or concept in our head. At any time during the day we can step through one of our breaths into a larger perspective and take a brief rest from the demands of our personality and its dramas.

If done regularly, Buddhist mindfulness meditation can make a profound difference in how we live and how we feel about our lives. If you are interested in pursuing this evolutionary sport, I suggest that you find a teacher or meditation center where you can study and deepen your understanding.

Finally, it has been said that the teachings of the Buddha are like a bird with two wings—one wing is wisdom and the other is compassion. The wings both grow out of mindfulness meditation practice, and they support each other in the flight toward self-realization. With every stroke of insight into our true nature comes a corresponding feeling of compassion for all beings with whom we share the conditions of our existence.

In Buddhist teaching, the development of the mind-states of com-passion (*karuna*) and loving-kindness (*metta*) are not moral command-ments but rather an organic outgrowth of wisdom. As we realize our own evolutionary nature we automatically begin to feel increasing kin-ship with all forms of life. All other animals become our cousins, grown from the same cells; all plant life is feeding us our oxygen nutrient and can be seen as our green umbilical cord to Mother Earth.

As we experience our basic human condition through the Four Foundations, we also come to realize how much we have in common with all other humans. We become aware that we share the same shape and moment in evolutionary history; we carry the same legacy of scars and triumphs, the same dreams and limitations, the same experiment in living. We have come alive together in what paleontologists call the Holocene. We are *epoch* mates, all sharing the same 'cene!

We realize that underneath the thin layers of personality we are joined together at the amygdala and the neocortex, at the thumb, and at the upright, forward-facing hip. We are all part of the same project, whether it be simple survival or some unknown purpose of a mysterious guiding intelligence. Meditation teaches us that we are human, and as some mystics say, "When we remember we are human we are praying."

Since we have so much in common, perhaps we could simply con-sider our journey toward self-realization in the plural. Instead of asking "Who am I?" the question could become "Who are *we?*" Our inquiry then becomes a community koan and we all immediately become great saints—called bodhisattvas in Buddhism—helping each other through this moment in the evolution of life on earth. In this evolutionary sport, we are all on the same team. All of us are Earthlings.

Acknowledgments

This book rests on the shoulders of all my teachers, reaching back to the Buddha and forward to those who have taught and inspired me in person, including Tsoknyi Rinpoche, H. W. L. Poonja, Anagarika Munindra, Ajahn Jumnien, S. N. Goenka, Joseph Goldstein, Joanna Macy, Jack Kornfield, and Sharon Salzberg.

I extend my deepest gratitude to the many people who helped me shape this book, including Shoshana Alexander, whose fine intellect and great heart helped me discover where I wanted to go and how to get there; Dr. Robert Fraser, for making the science list and checking it twice; Emeliana Pellouchoud and Dr. Alan Gevins, for a specific review of the brain matter; Dr. Mark Epstein for a psychological evaluation (of the book, not me); Dan Clurman for making sure that my computer and I remained friends; and Jack Kornfield for his constant encouragement and friendship.

I wish to acknowledge my colleagues at the *Inquiring Mind* for their support and friendship—my co-editor Barbara Gates for her editing skills and careful, tender ways, and Alan Novidor for his trustworthy guiding hand.

A huge thank you to Richard Grossinger and the team at Inner Traditions for their care and collaboration; to the incomparable Arnie Kotler for his expert guidance and friendship; to Kerry Nelson, Kim Criswell, and Paddy Sandino for all manner of support and consultation.

A special note of gratitude to my daughter Rose for her exceptional work on this book and the bright light she brings to my life every day.

I feel very privileged to be part of the flowering of Buddhadharma in the West—and I am especially honored to be part of the community of teachers and staff at both the Spirit Rock Meditation Center in Woodacre, California, and the Insight Meditation Society in Barre, Massachusetts. Also, my special thanks and regards to the Berkeley Wednesday night sitting group for inspiration and for being a sounding board for my ideas.

For many decades of tremendous insight, support, and affection, I thank Mudita Nisker, Steven Kaplan, Perry Garfinkel, Jeff Greenwald, Kevin Griffin, Nina Wise, Stan Grof, Ram Dass, Jane and James Baraz, Terry Vandiver, Djuna and Aidan, the Burtons, Michael Grove, the Neidorfs, Jan Buffum and family, and the poetry club. May you all live with ease of mind and lightness of heart.

References

The numbers given at left in the entries below are for the book pages where these quoted works can be found.

FOREWORD

xi. *The Lotus Sutra,* translated by Burton Watson (New York: Columbia Press, 1993), 32.

CHAPTER ONE.
A CASE OF MISTAKEN IDENTITY

8. The Buddha, *Samyutta Nikaya (The Book of the Kindred Sayings),* trans. Caroline A. F. Rhys Davids (Oxford: Pali Text Society, 1996).
8. Albert Einstein, *Ideas and Opinions* (New York: Three Rivers Press, 1954), 12.
10. Philip Cushman, *Constructing America, Constructing the Self* (New York: Addison-Wesley, 1995), 301.
11. Charles Taylor, *Sources of the Self* (Cambridge, Mass.: Harvard University Press, 1989), 28.
11. Julian Jaynes, *The Origin of Consciousness in the Breakdown of the Bicameral Mind* (Boston: Houghton Mifflin, 1976), 70, 72.
13. David Darling, *Zen Physics* (New York: HarperCollins, 1996), 177.
14. Alan Watts, *The Book: On the Taboo Against Knowing Who You Are* (New York: Vintage Books, 1972), 11.
15. Colin Tudge, The *Time Before History* (New York: Scribner, 1996), 14.
16. Joanna Macy, in conversation, September 1997.
17. Ken Wilber, *A Brief History of Everything* (Boulder, CO: Shambhala, 1996), 204.

17. Thich Nhat Hanh, The *Sun My Heart* (Berkeley, Calif.: Parallax Press, 1988), 101.

CHAPTER TWO.
THE BUDDHA WAS A BIOLOGIST

18. Francisco J. Varela, Evan Thompson, and Eleanor Rosch, *The Embodied Mind* (Cambridge, Mass.: The MIT Press, 1993), 22.
20. "The Abhidhamma," in *Abhidhamma Studies,* by Nyanaponika Thera (Kandy, Sri Lanka: Buddhist Publication Society, 1965), 45.
20. John Platt, The *Steps to Man* (New York: John Wiley and Sons, 1966), 185.
22. "The Four Noble Truths," as described in the "Mahasatipatthana Sutra," from the *Digha Nikaya: The Long Discourses of the Buddha,* trans. Maurice Walshe (Boston: Wisdom Publications, 1987), 344.
22. *The Dhammapada,* trans. Irving Babbitt (New York: New Directions, 1936), 14.

CHAPTER THREE. MINDFULNESS

28. "Mahasatipatthana Sutra: The Four Foundations of Mindfulness," from the *Digha Nikaya: The Long Discourses of the Buddha,* trans. Maurice Walshe (Boston: Wisdom Publications, 1987), 335.
32. Nyanaponika Thera, *The Heart of Buddhist Meditation* (London: Rider, 1962), 117.
32. Nyanaponika Thera, The *Heart of Buddhist Meditation: The Buddha's Way of Mindfulness* (Newburyport, MA: Red Wheel/Weiser, 2014), 157.

CHAPTER FOUR.
THE FIRST FOUNDATION OF MINDFULNESS

34. *Anguttara Nikaya (The Gradual Sayings),* trans. F. L. Woodward, (London: Pali Text Society, 1982).
35. *Anattalankkhana Sutta,* quoted in *Selfless Persons,* by Steven Collins (London: Cambridge University Press, 1982), 97.
38. Jack Kerouac, from his notebooks on display during traveling museum exhibit, "The Beats."

40. *Mahasatipatthana Sutra,* in *Digha Nikaya: The Long Discourses of the Buddha,* trans. Maurice Walshe (Boston: Wisdom Publications, 1987), 335–336.

40. Thich Nhat Hanh, from public talk, Berkeley Community Theater, Berkeley, Calif., 198 8. See also: *Breathe! You Are Alive* (Berkeley, Calif.: Parallax Press, 1996).

41. "Anapanasati Sutra: The Discourse on Full Awareness of Breathing," in *Majjhima Nikaya: The Middle Length Discourses of the Buddha,* trans. Bhikkhu Nanamoli and Bhikkhu Bodhi (Boston: Wisdom Publications, 1995), 941–948.

43. The Buddha's instructions quoted throughout Part I are all from the *Mahasatipatthana Sutra*: in *Digha Nikaya: The Long Discourses of the Buddha,* trans. Maurice Walshe, 335–338.

45. The Buddha's instructions quoted throughout Part I are all from the *Mahasatipatthana Sutra*: in *Digha Nikaya: The Long Discourses of the Buddha,* trans. Maurice Walshe, 335–338.

47. Henry David Thoreau, quoted in *Star Thrower,* by Loren Eiseley (New York: Harcourt Brace Jovanovich, 1978), 191.

48. Lynn Margulis and Dorion Sagan, *What Is Life?* (New York: Simon & Schuster, 1995), 28.

50. William Bryant Logan, *Dirt: The Ecstatic Skin of the Earth* (New York: Riverhead, 1995), 1

52. Colin Tudge, *The Time Before History* (New York: Scribner, 1996), 18.

53. Dogen, "The Mountains and Waters Sutra," in *Moon in a Dewdrop,* ed. Kazuaki Tanahashi (New York: Farrar, Straus and Giroux: North Point Press, 1985).

54. Yves Coppens, quoted in *The Origin of Humankind,* by Richard Leakey, (New York: Basic Books, 1994), 16.

57. D. H. Lawrence, "A Propos of Lady Chatterley's Lover," in *A Selection from Phoenix* (Middlesex, England: Penguin Books, 1971).

57. Buddhaghosa, *Visuddhimagga: The Path of Purification,* trans. Bhikkhu Nanamoli (Kandy, Sri Lanka: Buddhist Publication Society, 1991), xix, 617.

60. Lynn Margulis and Dorion Sagan, *Slanted Truths* (New York: Copernicus, 1997), 78.

60. Margulis and Sagan, *What Is Life?,* 49, 164.

61. Thich Nhat Hanh, *The Heart of Understanding* (Berkeley, Calif.: Parallax Press, 1988), 21.

61. Issa, *The Essential Haiku,* ed. Robert Hass (Hopewell, N.J.: Ecco Press, 1994), 170.

64. Carl Sagan, *The Demon-Haunted World* (New York: Random House, 1995), 330.

65. Lynn Margulis, "Vindicated Heretic," in *From Gaia to Selfish Genes: Selected Writings in the Life Sciences* (Cambridge, Mass.: The MIT Press, 1992), 50.

66. David Darling, *Zen Physics* (New York: HarperCollins, 1996) p. 12.

66. Lynn Margulis, *From Gaia to Selfish Genes,* 55.

67. Lynn Margulis and Dorion Sagan, "Microcosmos," in *From Gaia to Selfish Genes,* 59.

69. Jonathan Weiner, *The Beak of the Finch* (New York: Vintage Books, 1994), 279.

70. Richard Leakey, *The Origin of Humankind* (New York: Basic Books, 1994), 119.

71. Stephen Jay Gould, *Full House* (New York: Harmony Books, 1996), 140.

73. Niles Eldredge, foreword to *What Is Life?,* by Lynn Margulis and Dorion Sagan (New York: Simon & Schuster, 1995), 9.

73. Stephen Jay Gould, quoted in Margulis and Sagan, *What Is Life?,* 124.

75. Jack Kerouac, "Neal and the Three Stooges," *New Editions* 2, (1957).

76. Margulis and Sagan, *What Is Life?,* 123.

76. Margulis and Sagan, *What Is Life?,* 178.

77. Margulis and Sagan, *Slanted Truths,* 97.

78. Plato, *Phaedo* (Oxford: Oxford University Press, 1993).

78. "Mahaparinibbana Sutra," in *Digha Nikaya: The Long Discourses of the Buddha,* trans. Maurice Walshe (Boston: Wisdom Publications, 1987), 231.

79. "Mahasatipatthana Sutta," in *The Heart of Buddhist Meditation,* by Nyanaponika Thera, (London: Rider, 1962), 20.

81. Mark Twain, "Three Thousand Years Among the Microbes," in *The Devil's Race-Track,* ed. John S. Tuckey (Oakland: University of California Press, 1966), 175.

84. *Japanese Death Poems,* ed. Yoel Hoffmann (Rutland, Vermont: Charles E. Tuttle, 1986).

CHAPTER FIVE.
THE SECOND FOUNDATION OF MINDFULNESS

86. *Sutta-Nipata,* trans. H. Saddhatissa (Surrey, England: Curzon Press, 1985), 85.

87. "Mahasatipatthana Sutta," in *The Heart of Buddhist Meditation,* by Nyanaponika Thera (London: Rider, 1962), 121–122.

88. "Chachakka Sutta," in *Majjhima Nikaya: The Middle Length Discourses*

trans. Bhikkhu Nanamoli and Bhikkhu Bodhi (Boston: Wisdom Publications, 1995), 1129–1136.

89. Charles Darwin, from his early journals, quoted in *Star Thrower* by Loren Eiseley (New York: Harcourt Brace Jovanovich, 1978), 187.

91. Jon Franklin, *Molecules of the Mind* (New York: Dell, 1987), 222.

92. Robert M. Sapolsky, *Behave: The Biology of Humans at Our Best and Worst* (New York: Penguin Books, 2019), 23.

93. Franklin, *Molecules of the Mind,* 222.

94. *Sutta-Nipata*, 61.

97. Lama Anagarika Govinda, *The Psychological Attitude of Buddhist Philosophy* (London: Rider, 1969), 130.

99. Jon Kabat-Zinn, *Full Catastrophe Living* (New York: Delta, 1990).

109. Albert Camus, "An Absurd Reasoning" in *The Myth of Sisyphus and Other Essays* (New York: Vintage Books, 1955), 38.

CHAPTER SIX.
THE THIRD FOUNDATION OF MINDFULNESS

111. Loren Eiseley, *Star Thrower,* (New York: Harcourt Brace Jovanovich, 1978), 194.

111. Alan Watts, quoted in, *What Is Life?,* by Lynn Margulis and Dorion Sagan (New York: Simon & Schuster, 1995), 41.

112. Joseph LeDoux, *The Emotional Brain* (New York: Simon & Schuster, 1996), 17.

113. *Jara Sutta,* in *Sutta-Nipata,* trans. H. Saddhatissa (Surrey, England: Curzon Press, 1985), 96.

114. W. F. Jayasuriya, *The Psychology and Philosophy of Buddhism* (Kuala Lumpur, Malaysia: Buddhist Missionary Society, 1963), 3.

114. "The Dhammapada," in Jack Kornfield, ed. *Teachings of the Buddha* (Boulder, CO: Shambhala Publications, 2007), 44.

115. *Mahasatipatthana Sutra*, in *Digha Nikaya: The Long Discourses of the Buddha,* trans. Maurice Walshe (Boston: Wisdom Publications, 1987), 340.

116. *Samyutta Nikaya,* in *The Mind Like Fire Unbound* by Thanissaro Bhikkhu (Barre, Mass.: Dhamma Dana Publications, 1993), 80.

118. "Bhaddakaratta Sutra," in Kornfield, ed., *Teachings of the Buddha,* 115.

120. Daniel Goleman, *Emotional Intelligence* (New York: Bantam, 1995), 16.

123. Jon Franklin, *Molecules of the Mind* (New York: Dell, 1987), 259

124. Candace Pert, *Molecules of Emotion* (New York: Scribner, 1997), 23.

125. Robert Zajonc, quoted in *The Emotional Brain,* by Joseph LeDoux, (New York: Simon & Schuster, 1996), 53.

127. Margulis and Sagan, *What Is Life?,* 32.

128. Daniel Goleman, *Emotional Intelligence,* 47.

129. *Sutta-Nipata,* 86.

130. Jerome Kagan, *Galen's Prophecy* (New York: Basic Books, 1994), xxii.

134. "Samyutta Nikaya," in *Selfless Persons,* by Steven Collins (London: Cambridge University Press, 1982), 101.

135. Buddhaghosa, *Visuddhimagga: The Path of Purification,* trans. Bhikkhu Nanamoli (Kandy, Sri Lanka: Buddhist Publication Society, 1991), 75–103.

138. Rumi, *Unseen Rain,* trans. John Moyne and Coleman Barks (Putney, Vermont: Threshold Books, 1986), 63.

138. James Hillman, from the foreword to *Ecopyschology,* by Theodore Roszak (San Francisco: Sierra Club Books, 1995)

139. Norman O. Brown, *Love's Body* (New York: Vintage Books, 1968), 98.

140. Carl Jung, in *The Secret of the Golden Flower,* trans. Richard Wilhelm (New York: Harcourt Brace and World, Inc., 1962), 93.

140. Dr. Mark Epstein, *Thoughts without a Thinker* (New York: Basic Books, 1995), 52.

141. Otto Rank, quoted in Epstein, *Thoughts without a Thinker,* 52.

141. Daniel Brown, quoted in *MindScience: An East-West Dialogue* (Boston: Wisdom Publications, 1991), 101.

143. Tulku Thondup, *The Healing Power of Mind* (Boulder, CO: Shambhala, 1996), 77.

144. *Visuddhimagga,* 141.

144. "Visuddhimagga," in Bhikkhu Bodhi, ed., *The Vision of Dhamma: Buddhist Writings of Nyanaponika Thera* (Onalaska, WA: Pariyatti Publishing, 2000), 100.

147. Lama Anagarika Govinda, *The Psychological Attitude of Buddhist Philosophy* (London: Rider, 1969), 63.

150. Thich Nhat Hanh, "Breathing into Politics," in *Inquiring Mind,* 12, no. 2 (Spring 1996).

153. "Anapanasati Sutra: The Discourse on Full Awareness of Breathing," in *Majjhima Nikaya: The Middle Length Discourses of the Buddha,* trans. Bhikkhu Nanamoli and Bhikkhu Bodhi (Boston: Wisdom Publications, 1995), 941–948.

153. Thich Nhat Hanh, *Touching Peace* (Berkeley, Calif.: Parallax Press, 1992), 12.

CHAPTER SEVEN.
THE FOURTH FOUNDATION OF MINDFULNESS

155. "The Dhammapada," in Kornfield, ed., *Teachings of the Buddha*, 4.

156. Tulku Urgyen Rinpoche, *Rainbow Painting* (Hong Kong: Rangjung Yeshe Publications), 53.

158. Charles Darwin, in *Darwin on Man*, ed. Howard E. Gruber (New York: E. P. Dutton & Co., 1974).

158. Marvin Minsky, *The Society of Mind* (New York: Touchstone Books, 1988).

158. Richard M. Restak, *Brainscapes* (New York: Hyperion, 1995).

159. Daniel C. Dennett, *Consciousness Explained* (Boston: Back Bay Books, 1991).

159. Daniel Dennett, *Elbow Room* (Cambridge, Mass.: The MIT Press, 1984).

159. Rodolfo Llinas, quoted in Restak, *Brainscapes*, 90.

160. Francisco J. Varela, Evan Thompson, and Eleanor Rosch, *The Embodied Mind* (Cambridge, Mass.: The MIT Press, 1993), 28.

163. Minsky, *The Society of Mind*, 63.

163. Explanations of *Abhidhamma* views found in *A Comprehensive Manual of Abhidhamma,* ed. Bhikkhu Bodhi (Kandy, Sri Lanka: Buddhist Publication Society, 1993).

167. Michael I. Posner and Marcus E. Raichle, *Images of Mind* (New York: Scientific American Library, 1994).

168. Restak, *Brainscapes*, 35.

168. Ray Jackendoff, *Consciousness and the Computational Mind* (Cambridge, Mass.: The MIT Press, 1987).

169. Ajahn Chah, *A Still Forest Pool* (Wheaton, Ill.: The Theosophical Publication Society, 1985),

169. Chah, *A Still Forest Pool,* 17.

170. Walpola Rahula, *What the Buddha Taught* (New York: Grove Press, 1959), 66.

171. "Mahatanhasamkhaya Sutta," in *Selfless Persons,* by Steven Collins (London: Cambridge University Press, 1982), 103.

172. Lama Anagarika Govinda, *The Psychological Attitude of Buddhist Philosophy* (London: Rider, 1969), 140.

174. Dogen, "Actualizing the Fundamental Point," in *Moon in a Dewdrop,* ed. Kazuaki Tanahashi (New York: Farrar, Straus and Giroux/North Point Press, 1985), 70.

179. Nyoshul Khenpo, *Natural Great Perfection* (Boulder, CO: Shambhala/ Snow Lion, 1995), 78.

179. Shabkar Lama, *The Flight of the Garuda* (Boston: Wisdom Publications, 1994), 104.

180. Tulku Urgyen, *Rainbow Painting*, 53.

181. Varela, Thompson, and Rosch, *Embodied Mind*, 80.

182. Ken Wilber, *A Brief History of Everything* (Boulder, CO: Shambhala, 1996), 42.

184. Shabkar Lama, *The Flight of the Garuda*, 128.

Index

About the Author

WES "SCOOP" NISKER is an award-winning broadcast journalist and commentator, a respected Buddhist meditation teacher, a bestselling author, and a standup Dharma comic who has been described (in the *New York Times*) as "masterful at using humor to lighten the enlightenment journey." His signature signoff at San Francisco's KSAN radio was "If you don't like the news, go out and make some of your own." Wes Nisker's other books include the enduring classic *The Essential Crazy Wisdom* and *The Big Bang, the Buddha, and the Baby Boom.* He was founding coeditor of *The Inquiring Mind,* an international Buddhist journal, and he continues to lead retreats and workshops at Spirit Rock Meditation Center and worldwide. He lives in Oakland, California.